For my mother

Return to;
    Mrs. Russell Gilbert
    2773 - 7th St
    Livermore, Calif.

Confessions of Mrs. Smith

ALSO BY ELINOR GOULDING SMITH

The Complete Book of Absolutely Perfect Housekeeping
The Complete Book of Absolutely Perfect Baby and Child Care

Confessions of
Mrs. Smith RECKLESS

RECOLLECTIONS, TRUE & OTHERWISE

BY Elinor Goulding Smith

Drawings by Roy Doty

Harcourt, Brace and Company ⊞ New York

Contents

Memoirs of a Clotheshorse

Memoirs of a Clotheshorse

I'm the one who always stands out in a crowd. See that crowd over there at the party? See all those women in off-the-shoulder *peau de soie?* Now see that one in the corner in a sweater and skirt? That's me.

I'll kill myself. I think I'll cut my throat. Oh well, life is too short to fuss over such trivialities. After all, it isn't what you wear, it's what you do that counts.

See the people at the suburban dinner party? See all the women in those smart tailored suits? Now see the one on the right in a strapless emerald green satin sheath? That's me.

Why should I cut my throat? What difference does it make? In a hundred years nobody will even know about it. If you're neat and well groomed, that's all that matters, isn't it? Besides, gas will be neater.

Oh this is silly. Why should I turn on the gas? No one is noticing me. It doesn't even matter what I wear. Well, why aren't they noticing me? I'm just as good as they are, aren't I? What's wrong with me all of a sudden? I'm a human being too, you know.

Sometimes I try outguessing them. Now then, I say to myself cheerfully, let's take it easy and let's not get in a panic. We'll just figure this thing out sensibly. Now tonight, for instance. Let's see. It's just dinner at a friend's house in the suburbs. They probably won't have more than one other couple. I know them to be very informal people. It's a weekday night. For sure this is a wool dress evening, with pearls just to show it's not like marketing. All right now, wool dress. But let's take into consideration one more factor which is that I am always wrong and see what we come up with. That would make it a good black silk and high-heeled sandals evening. But if I wear the silk and high heels, they'll absolutely have to be wearing sweaters. Maybe I should go in a bathing suit and be frankly wrong? Or perhaps I could dress up as Madame Defarge or Medusa? Maybe after all I should just stay home and go to bed. I could tell them I broke my leg this afternoon.

I think I'll take poison. I finally ended up in the wool dress, and there were eight couples, all the women in bouffant taffeta and pale blue lace sheaths.

Oh that's ridiculous. You don't kill yourself because you wore the wrong thing once. They weren't talking about you behind your back. They were probably talking about their sister-in-law or the president of the PTA. Why would they talk about you? Well, why shouldn't they talk about me? I'm somebody.

Oh how silly. They don't care what I wear. They're my *friends*. Why don't they care what I wear? They care what they wear, don't they? We're not savages who just wear clothes to keep out the drafts. We're supposed to be civilized, and clothes are supposed to be an adornment. Also they're supposed to show that you have a sense of style, that you have chic, that above all, oh my God, you know what's done and what isn't done on a given occasion. I'll throw myself out of the window.

4

Now let's be sensible. It's much more important to have a sense of the importance of things than a sense of style or chic or being able to tell a bathrobe from a hat. Now take Saturday night. Dinner for forty people at eight o'clock. This one is easy. You can't wear a sweater and skirt to a dinner party on a Saturday night for forty people. But I won't dress up too much either. You don't want to overdo these things. It's more sophisticated to be a little underdressed than a little overdressed. So let's see. The blue taffeta with a low neck but long sleeves? That should do it.

See that crowd there at that dinner party? See all those women in smart little black suits? Now see that one over there in low-necked blue taffeta? That's me.

But I'm not going to throw myself out of the window anyway. I'm going to hold my breath till I turn blue.

On second thought I won't hold my breath either. I'll just stand there and smile bravely as though nothing happened. After all, good manners are more important than clothes. Aren't they?

Anyway, tomorrow is another day. Now *what* shall I wear tomorrow? It's a little party for the teacher who is getting married, just an informal little tea at one of the mothers' houses to present the teacher with the sterling silver parsley server from all the children in the class. The party is right after school, the temperature is ninety-two. I'll do it. I'll go as a . . . no, no. I'll dress as nicely as I can so I won't disgrace my children in front of all the other mothers.

See those ladies at that tea? See the lovely party dresses with scoop necks and bows and sashes and sleeves? See the silk stockings and the high-heeled

5

pumps? Now see that woman cowering behind a tall lamp in a nice clean cotton wash dress and a pair of flat sandals? That's me. Always neat. I'll fall on my sword.

"You must come for the weekend," says the friend, "to this *darling* little hotel we've discovered miles from nowhere. You don't have to pack *anything*. It's very informal. Just bring a bathing suit."

See that darling little informal hotel out there? See the little informal country dining room? See how casual it is? Look how casually the six hundred ladies throw their mink coats back off their shoulders, revealing their lovely pale blue satin and their diamond necklaces. Now see that very casual one over there throwing an old tweed coat around *very* casually? That's me. I'll hit my head against a wall till I drop dead.

I'm meeting friends in the city. We're to go to the Metropolitan and look at pictures and then have lunch. This is easy. You *have* to be comfortable for that.

See those ladies strolling around the Early Flemish room? Don't they look nice? Suits nipped at the waist, furry bulky hats, alligator opera pumps and bags, hand-stitched beige gloves. Now see that lady a few steps behind them in shoes so comfortable she has to shuffle to keep them on, clothes that sort of hang down loosely, no hat, no gloves, and very comfortable hair? You guessed it. I'll drop dead.

No I won't. I won't give them the satisfaction. I'll go home and fix supper for my family.

See that family eating supper in the kitchen? There are two little boys in dungarees and flannel shirts. There is a father in corduroy slacks and an old jersey. See that

6

mother dishing up spaghetti? That's me. *They* don't notice what I'm wearing. It could be pale pink pleated chiffon or a burlap sack for all they care. And here I am in a new dress. I'll kill myself in the morning.

Sleek, Chic . . . Eek!

I can't understand why none of the smart fashion magazines has been around to do a feature on me. I can only assume that there has been an awful oversight and I have worked out some ideas for a really nice long article when they do come.

The first picture shows the family at breakfast, and the caption should be something like this: "The Robert Smiths breakfast with their famous informality. Son Joseph is in the Babee-Tenda, son Daniel seated on the step stool at the kitchen table. The gracious Mrs. Robert Paul Smith (the former Miss Elinor Goulding, graduate of P.S. 6) stirs the Pablum while the coffee boils over merrily on the range. Mrs. Smith, who is known for the chic informality of her skirts and shirts, likes for early morning wear a gray crinkled cotton skirt with a pristine white T-shirt. Mr. Smith squeezes the orange juice in an old pair of tan slacks which he wears with a careless authority. The Smiths' kitchen combines the smart sleekness of green Formica counter tops with a gay clutter of toys, while the green-and-white linoleum is brightened up with dashes of ketchup red and deep spinach."

The second picture might show me walking to the village with the children, and the caption might be: "Mrs. Smith walks to the village with son Joseph (in the stroller) and son Daniel (under her feet). Always individual, Mrs. Smith prefers to walk on the sidewalk. For an afternoon's shopping with the children she likes a gray crinkled cotton skirt with a white T-shirt. The shirt is enlivened, for afternoon wear, with a dash of Clapp's Junior Carrot at the shoulder, while the gray skirt sports a bold design of harmonizing Swift's Strained Beef Liver. One skirt pocket is daringly torn down the side, making the jutting line at the hip that Paris is so mad about this season. Mrs. Smith's ineffably chic, close-cropped hair, cut with a straight bang across the forehead, looks as though it might have been cut by the little boys' barber. (It looks that way because it was.) She also wears, with great style, a wrinkled brow. She wonders if she turned off the oven."

The next picture should be something like this: "The Robert Smiths, with sons Daniel (on trike) and Joseph (in playpen), enjoy a summer afternoon on the roomy old-fashioned porch of their charming home in Scarsdale, New York. Mrs. Smith (the former Miss Elinor Goulding of Manhattan and the Julia Richman High School) likes Pittsburgh's Florhide Paint in Pewter Gray for her porch, and for fun-at-home she likes her smartly casual gray crinkled cotton skirt and white T-shirt. Here the charming Mrs. Smith expertly wields the 1½-inch brush, while Mr. Smith (who wears an old pair of tan slacks with his inimitable air of authority) hogs the

8

3-inch brush. Note the porch of this unusual home, which is placed—for the utmost in summer comfort—*outside* the house."

The next picture shows a Sunday afternoon in the back yard: "Mr. Robert Smith is in the swimming pool, set in back of their charming home in Scarsdale, New York, with sons Daniel (standing) and Joseph (on all fours). Mr. Smith wears, with an easy casual authority, an old pair of tan shorts. Daniel and Joseph wear, with a flair, nothing at all. Mrs. Robert Smith (the former Miss Elinor Goulding of New York City and the Interboro Institute of Secretarial Training) gathers in the wash, and *loves* her gray crinkled cotton skirt and white T-shirt. The Smiths like to entertain gay crowds of young people around the pool on hot afternoons. (It's a cinch they couldn't do it *in* a pool 48 inches in diameter.)"

Then there might be a picture showing the Smiths entertaining guests in the evening, and I suggest the following caption: "Mr. and Mrs. Smith entertain guests in the living room of their charming home in Scarsdale, New York. At the Smith home, where the unexpected prevails, guests sit on chairs or the sofa with a deliciously gay and hilarious informality. Mrs. Robert Smith (the former Miss Elinor Goulding of Manhattan, the Bronx, Brooklyn, Queens, and Richmond), who is known for her sudden changes of mood in dress, likes for informal evening wear a *green* crinkled cotton skirt and a *yellow* T-shirt. Her immaculate grooming (she has washed) and the faint perfume of Tabu mingled with Loin Lamb Chop complete the gracious picture. Who but the Smiths, who are known among their friends for unusual little late suppers, would serve coffee and cake for surprise value?

"Mrs. Smith collects antique silver polish and Early American Glass Wax, while Mr. Smith is an avid and devoted collector of mellow old American pine cones and cherry pits."

My Headstrong Feet

I don't remember when my trouble with shoes first started. All I know is that as far back as I can remember my feet have simply not fit into shoes. Nevertheless I *did* wear shoes for many years, because my family maintained the old-fashioned idea that it doesn't "look nice" to go around barefoot.

Now there is nothing particularly wrong with my feet. To look at them, you'd never suspect a thing. They appear to be quite ordinary, with five toes on each in the usual arrangement. They are quite happy in sneakers, slippers, moccasins, sandals, and huaraches. And I have no doubt they'd feel grand in *geta* and *sabots,* too. But just put shoes on them for five minutes and everything happens. My arches fall, my toes hurt, blisters come on my heel, corns appear on my toes, athlete's foot develops, and it all burns and aches.

As soon as I walk into a shoe store, they switch all the sizes. Whatever size I wore the last time is all wrong this time. Not that it matters much, though, because whatever I end up with hurts so much that after a few days I give them to the Salvation Army or anybody who'll take them and go back to my sloppy old sandals. The shoe salesman is always optimistic. "Of course we can fit you," he says without hesitation. "Fitting the difficult foot is our specialty." Then he measures my feet and smiles happily. "Very narrow heel," he says, "that's your trouble. You need a combination last." And he goes off confidently to get the shoes. When I try them on his confidence soon wilts, for the combination last rubs the heel, crushes the toes, presses on the instep, and sets up a general aching and throbbing. Within a few minutes the salesman is a muttering wreck and goes off to get drunk. I limp home. Naturally I can never go to the same shoe store more than once.

As a matter of fact I wouldn't mind all this, because I'm so happy in my sandals and slippers and things. But although I can get away with it all right in the summer, it's not so good in the middle of winter. Not that *I* mind. I'd much rather have my toes frozen than crushed, but nobody else can stand it. I'm slopping happily down the street, singing gaily to myself as the snow and sleet squush in my shoes, but my husband winces. "For God's sake," he says, "can't you wear shoes like everybody else? You'll get pneumonia going around like that." As a matter of fact, all I ever got is a head cold I caught from the children, and it's a lucky thing I'm so comfortable in my sandals when I'm running up and down stairs with trays while I nurse my husband and children through their winter grippe and flu and bronchitis.

Actually, I don't always look as though I've just

stepped out of a Saks Fifth Avenue window anyway, but I can, when the occasion calls for it, appear at least reasonably neat, well groomed and within a year or so of the latest fashion. That is, all but the Feet. The feet have a strong tendency to go their own sloppy way, dressed for the wrong season, the wrong occasion, and in the wrong color. This is not entirely my fault. It happens occasionally that a particularly comfortable and favorite pair of sandals comes apart entirely. In the spring or summer, they can be replaced. If it should happen in January, things are not so simple. I trudge from store to store, begging for any old sandals left over from the previous summer. The salesmen are kind, recognizing that I am the victim of some strange aberration that I cannot control, but all they have left is a size 4B in Kelly green, when what I need is practically any size *but* 4B in red. That is how it sometimes happens that I turn up in the city for dinner and the theater quite nicely put together, hair combed neatly, fingernails clean, lipstick not smudged, and on my feet a pair of old purple sandals with one strap broken; plus, of course, a husband trying hard to look as though he doesn't know me.

It is the opinion of my Aunt Sophie, who also has foot troubles, that American shoe manufacturers make shoes the wrong shape. With this opinion I concur.

Oh well, I'm sitting here wiggling my toes, my feet cool and comfortable, in an old pair of yellow sandals with a big hole in the sole. *I'm* happy.

Hats I Have Worn

I didn't wear anything on my head when I was a baby, but by the time I was two or three, I was wearing hats regularly. In the spring there was the large-brimmed navy blue straw with long ribbon streamers down the back, and in the fall there was the large-brimmed tan beaver felt with brown ribbon streamers down the back. The former was worn with a plain, strictly tailored navy blue coat, the latter with a plain brown chinchilla coat with a small beaver collar. As my sister and I and my two girl cousins all wore identical hats and coats, I naturally believed those to be the only kinds of hats and coats there were, and I was, incidentally, the constant target of outgrown ones. On the grand and rare occasions when I did acquire a new hat or coat, it seemed to me that my mother ought simply to be able to phone the store where she'd bought the previous ones and say, "*Now* send it along in size *4*." But oddly enough, providing my sister and me with those hats and coats entailed shopping tours that were not considered complete unless they included Altman's, Best's, McCreery's, Oppenheim Collins', Gimbel's, Macy's, Lord and Taylor's, Arnold Constable's, Stern's, and Wanamaker's. In each store countless coats and hats had to be tried on, pulled on, pushed on, patted, yanked, pinched, pinned in, pinned up, taken off, sent home for my father to see, and then, most of them, sent back again.

The year-in, year-out custom of large round hats with streamers came to an abrupt end when my grandmother took up crocheting. I was about seven at the time, my sister ten, and we were the dismayed recipients of a steady stream—no, more a tidal wave—of crocheted hats. These hats were made of an especially scratchy wool in a peculiarly unbecoming shade of greenish tan. In shape they were more like tea cosies or warming-pan covers, and for decoration they had two large balls of wool that dangled at one side and bumped our ears. It was my belief that these hats were socks or mittens which had gotten out of control. My mother made us wear them so that Grandma's feelings wouldn't be hurt. Nobody thought about *our* feelings.

We got back at my mother the year she had typhoid fever and was still too weak when spring came to do any shopping. Grandma, by then, had gone on to afghans, and my aunt was assigned the task of buying my sister and me our new spring hats. On the way downtown my sister convinced her that we were *always* allowed to select our own hats. We then ran amok in Macy's Girls' Hats and promptly and decisively chose the two hats that were Most Likely to Remain Unsold.

My sister's was of a virulent color known as henna that was rampant that year. It was straw, lined with an even fiercer henna silk, and while generally pot-shaped, it rose to a high peak at the crown and was topped by a big henna bow. I was doubtful, but she said it was the most stunning hat she ever saw, and in this she was probably right. *Mine* was pale green straw, bonnet-shaped, and had a pink silk lining and lots of flowers and cherries. My aunt was a little pale, but we were flushed with pleasure and excitement.

My mother had a slight setback when she saw the hats, but by then it was too late to do anything about it, and on Easter Sunday we wore them proudly out strolling with my father. It was windy that Easter, and my sister's hat blew off and was crushed beyond recognition by a trolley car. I clutched mine fearfully, and by the time we got home, it was quite hopelessly out of shape. As soon as my mother was strong enough, she rushed us downtown again, and after a prolonged search she found two large navy blue hats with ribbon streamers.

Perhaps after that she thought we were grown up enough for real hats, or perhaps the big ones had gone out of style, but at any rate the next year we were the happy wearers of small, infinitely chic (we thought) cloche hats which covered our heads right down to the eyelids. This was especially fortunate for me, as I had one large new chicken-pox scar right in the center of my forehead. I also had a burn mark on my nose which resulted from my father's enthusiastic application of stale iodine to the place where a little girl in school had stuck me with her pen point, and my mother tried to make the cloche hat cover that too. I had to walk with my head back to see out.

Fortunately both of these disfigurements disappeared in time for off-the-face hats. At this time, for some reason, we patronized a kind of store that flourished then, where they cut and draped hats right on your head. It was exciting, because you never knew what was going to be the outcome, but with my mother standing by saying nervously, "I want it very youthful," somehow the outcomes were all pretty much the same: Disappointing.

One time though I announced firmly that I intended to have a hat which was *the* thing that year. It was brimless in front but had a long thing hanging around the sides and back, like an Egyptian hairdress. I must have been ten or eleven then, and my mother was just as firm that the hat must have a nice youthful style with a turned-up brim. The result was a compromise, but hardly neat. It fulfilled both demands by having a turned-up brim in front, and yet a suggestion of a thing hanging around the back, bumping my coat collar. I wore this hat hopefully for a time, thinking that perhaps no one noticed the brim in front, but later hopefully thought no one noticed the whole hat, as it was evident even to me that that hat was a mongrel.

The next summer I was away at camp, happily wearing faded green poplin bloomers and a white middy blouse with a green tie, when the Empress Eugénie hat burst on a startled world. We girls, at an age when we were beginning to sew our middy blouses down the sides to make them fit and daringly cutting sun-tan backs out of our bathing suits, were vehemently opposed to the Eugénie. "Now *who*," we said as we pored over the Sunday papers, "would be found dead in a thing like that?" A few weeks later, back in New York, we were knocking down old ladies in our rush to get Eugénie hats. Mine was brown felt, and while it was featherless, it definitely came to a point over my right eye, and had a large flat bow in the back that gave it the coveted shape. I could hardly bear to go indoors the first few weeks.

After the Eugénie broke the ice and I was old enough to buy my own hats, things were less exciting.

Now I have two little boys, who just wear knitted wool caps in the winter and crew cuts in the summer. Every once in a while when everybody has colds in the head and it's winter and the bank account has hit a new low and the oil burner suddenly refuses to function, I go out and buy the most expensive feather hat I can find, tuck it away carefully in tissue paper, and wish I had a place to wear it. But no hat, no matter how expensive, will ever be quite as exciting as the pale green straw with the pink lining and the flowers and cherries. *That* was a *hat*.

How I Acquired My Lack of Poise

The Prize Package

⌐▥▥▷ I was born the wrong sex and with a head of hair that was a mistake from the word go. It seemed to my worried parents that as a baby I was a flop and they thought my chance of marriage was small, but as I got older this optimism diminished.

When I was born I had a three-year-old sister with blonde wavy hair that always stayed in place. On her the hair ribbons sat smartly on top of her head, perky and crisp. On me they slid down the side and got crumpled and limp from being pulled and tugged about to get them on top again. I looked as though I was dragging around some Roman-striped seaweed, but if nothing else I had a certain air of insouciance.

My earliest memory is of my mother standing over me in the bathroom wielding a wet comb and clucking discouragedly as she tried to make a curl on top of my head. To this day nobody has yet succeeded in making a curl on my head. Many a hairdresser has gone all to pieces, but I myself keep cheerful. Sometimes I keep so cheerful that I have been known to comb my hair muttering hardly any curses from behind my clenched teeth.

When I say that I was born the wrong sex, this was not my own opinion. I didn't want to form any opinion at all till I saw how things worked out. It was the opinion of my father, who was thoroughly annoyed with my sister and me for turning out to be girls when he so specially wanted boys.

Faced with the unalterable and deplorable fact that my sister and I were girls, my father was nonetheless determined that we be what he called "good, all-round athletes." This was unfortunate because my sister was a small fragile girl who couldn't squeeze the toothpaste tube by herself, and I was a large fragile girl who wasn't any help. I liked to curl up by a warm radiator and read *The Little Princess* or sew dresses for my dolls with tiny stitches. On very active days I made soft peanut brittle and hard fudge.

Of course that's all very well now that I'm old enough so that nobody expects me to go romping around, but when I was a little girl, somebody was always nudging me with a tennis racquet or a basketball. The only things I really liked to do that involved any muscles at all were to ride my bicycle and to go roller skating, and those were the two things I wasn't allowed to do on the grounds that I was certain to be run over.

In addition to being forbidden to ride my bicycle (I still haven't figured out why they bought me the damn thing in the first place) and roller skates, I was also forbidden to jump rope. The ban on rope jumping had nothing to do with automobiles, however. Along with the hair, I was born with a heart murmur which causes some doctors to turn pale and turn in their stethoscopes. As I am now thirty-nine, it seems likely that those who said I'd never live to be twenty-one were mistaken. Be that as it may, the consensus was that I should not indulge in any violent exercise but that I was to lead a normal life otherwise. My father was torn between concern over this heart murmur and concern over my athletic ability. The result was that I would be forbidden, say, to overtire myself with embroidery but urged to go horseback riding once a week. It was confusing.

When I say that my father was concerned about this heart murmur, I did not mean to say "my father and mother." My mother is never really concerned about illness of any sort until the sick person has been laid out in his coffin, whereupon she goes to the funeral parlor and concedes that in this case something may really be wrong after all. My sister and I were always assumed by her to be malingering until the spots actually appeared or the X-ray showed the bone to be broken right apart in two separate pieces, and no matter what was wrong with us we were shooed off to school in the morning on the happy theory that it would all disappear by lunchtime. Once I took a piano lesson with a broken arm but it was not especially successful. My father took the opposite view and was certain that every scratch was a source of blood poisoning, every stomach ache indicated a ruptured appendix, and tetanus, typhoid, and botulism lurked everywhere.

In spite of the lamentable presence of germs and the even more lamentable heart murmur, I went off to camp in the summers, burdened to the Plimsoll line with athletic equipment and exhortations to develop a good tennis stroke and work at my basketball but not to tire myself out with nature walks and weaving. Nobody consulted me. The fact was that heart murmur or no heart murmur, I could no more play tennis than a fish. I was curiously gifted with an incredible ineptness at anything resembling sports. The minute I saw a tennis racquet I went all over limp, while the sight of a baseball simply made me duck. However, the rules said you had to, so I appeared on the appropriate court at the appropriate time, where I stood around nonchalantly and picked mosquito bite scabs. In spite of my nonchalance, I sprained my wrist on the tennis court, broke my nose on the basketball court, and broke three fingers on the baseball diamond. (Actually I didn't break my own nose. It was broken by a girl named Laurette, although I don't think she actually *meant* to break it. What she did mean to do when she slammed her elbow into my nose I can't imagine.) I still have the bump on my nose, but it was worth it because after that everybody looked the other way while I sneaked off and had a happy time making lopsided clay pots. My parents did not consider that the broken nose in any way improved my chance of finding a husband.

At college all students were given a thorough physical examination the first week, and I passed mine with flying colors. My Wassermann was negative, my vision 20-20, my red cell count high, and my tuberculin test created some little enthusiastic comment. I was *perfect.* All but two little things: One, my spine was in the shape of a letter S (Gothic), and Two, my heart made them look sharply to see if I was still there. I was, and I was promptly assigned to a cardiac gym class, during the course of which I was also to be given corrective exercises for my spine. (This spine, incidentally, is still giving satisfactory service, but X-ray technicians recoil the first time they encounter it and fear they've made a picture of some old bicycle parts by mistake.) I was in for cardiac gym and forbidden to do social dancing but was not excused from outdoor sports, indoor sports, or interpretive dancing.

I went once to the cardiac gym class out of sheer curiosity. It sounded pale and interesting. I assume that all the other unfortunates who turned up were in the same hazardous condition as I. First we were told to walk around the gym briskly. It was a very large gym used by the ROTC for army maneuvers and the pace was brisk indeed. At the end of the trip I was winded and felt sure that if I had never before been a cardiac case I was about to become one now. We were told to go around once more but this time to put a little pep into it. We did. I was puffing noticeably and seemed to be listing slightly to starboard. On the third trip we trotted. I could feel my bow sinking. I decided the doctors had been right after all.

I was going down fast when I was given my first exercise to straighten my spine. It was not difficult. I stepped up on a ladder, grasped a horizontal bar above my head, the ladder was removed, and I was told to stay there till further notice. It was during this exercise that I decided once and for all that gym (be it cardiac or not cardiac) was not for me, and should I ever again get down from that bar, which seemed doubtful, I would, in the interest of survival, take up breathing as my only sport.

My father was convinced that no decent, hearty, red-blooded American boy would think of marrying a girl who didn't play a *good game of tennis,* do a really *strong Australian crawl kick,* or wasn't a *capable horsewoman.* He was therefore resigned to my wasting away to a hollow-chested, round-shouldered, puny spinsterhood, and he was astonished when some years later a man actually did marry me. My mother, on the other hand, while not actively opposed to athletics, was more concerned about the condition of my hair which was still poor. Destitute, really. She had tried hot olive oil treatments, interspersed with singeing, violet ray, massage, and imprecations, but no matter what she did, it remained perfectly straight, dull brown (mouse, she preferred to call it), and completely inert. It had no *life* to it, she complained, as though hair was supposed to get up and run around. So when this man I spoke of came around and allowed as how he was willing to take me even in my own hair, she was just as astonished as my father.

Besides being a girl, with my hair, and being a non-athlete of the worst sort, other things had happened to make me, in their view, even less marriageable (had that been possible) than before.

I had left college under a tiny cloud. This little cloud had nothing to do with my grades, which were excellent, or my behavior, which was lovely. It seemed that nice Cornell girls did not appear on campus (where there were men) without stockings, even if they *did* have a sunburn and gangrene setting in on the backs of their knees. Nice Cornell girls did not slide down the hill on their rear even if the hill *was* covered with ice and they fell. And above all, nice Cornell girls did not skip their cardiac gym classes.

26

So I went home. My mother and father, along with all their other worries, were now saddled with this daughter who had no college degree and would *never* find a husband.

I got a job as a demonstrator for a twenty-five-cent perfume company and I demonstrated it in Liggett's Drugstore in Grand Central Station. I don't *think* there was any particular connection between my getting the job and the company going broke. Lots of companies went broke in those days. It wasn't terribly good perfume anyway. It came in three smells: gardenia, lilac, and sandalwood, and it was a kind of cream in a little flat plastic container. The theory was that you would stand right in the aisle with your foot sticking out and snag people who were racing through the store with three suitcases trying to catch a train, unless the lady across the aisle who was selling a liniment for sore aching muscles snagged them first. I didn't sell an awful lot of perfume, but I came home at night reeking of three kinds of twenty-five-cent perfume and everybody in the family fought over who would have to sit next to me at dinner. My parents didn't think it was too good a start on a career for a girl who wasn't very likely to get married.

The next job I got I really only got through pull. I sold ladies' belts at Bloomingdale's and they told me right from the beginning they didn't think I was a very aggressive salesgirl. They only hired me, they said frankly, because my mother was a buyer there and they were embarrassed to say no. Actually in me they had a jewel if they had only realized it. I may not have sold many belts, but I lent tone to the whole first floor by my quiet gracious manner. I will admit that while I was being gracious and charming that other girl sold three or four hundred dollars' worth of belts *in a very rude manner,* and when I turned in my book at night with totals of eighteen dollars and twenty-nine cents it didn't look good. Some people were bound to think she was a better salesgirl than I was. I would have sold more belts if I hadn't spent so much time in the employees' washroom crying into the roller towel because the customers were impatient. And all the time I was crying, that treacherous other girl kept right on selling belts and making herself look good.

We had a cash register and I never could remember to stand back. I had bruises where the little drawer hit me. Once in a while I remembered to back up first, but then got my finger caught in the drawer while slamming it professionally closed. I was professional at all times.

When it happened that we didn't have the right size belt in stock, we were supposed to take a larger one and cut it down to fit the customer. This took a lot of arguing because often the customer feared that this operation would ruin the belt. One day a lady came in and asked for a narrow gold belt in size twenty-eight. We didn't have one, so I took a thirty-two, sterilized my instruments, and prepared to operate. I took the punch and the little metal things you stuck in and the scissors for cutting off the extra piece, and I measured it all carefully, punched neatly, and when it was all done (and *beautifully*) I cut off the wrong piece and stood there holding the buckle and a little piece of belt about four inches long. The customer was discouraged and I blushed, but I hid the whole thing and found another one and set to work again. This time I worked slowly and carefully, determined not to make a mistake and trying hard not to be rattled by the phalanx of angry customers charging the counter with their plumes flying and their spears and shields at the ready. I held up the belt, grasped the scissors, and cut. This time I was left with a buckle and a little piece of gold kid belt about six inches long. I bit my lip, but game to the end, I went on with a third narrow gold belt. I went down fighting, remnants of belt still clutched in my fist.

Stern Brothers was the next lucky recipient of my talents. I'm not sure what my talents were, but no matter. The job for which I was hired required little in the way of talent. It needed no particular strength, agility, brains, looks, grammar, manual dexterity, or knowledge of the Greek classics, which was lucky because I had no knowledge of the Greek classics anyway. All you had to do, really, was be willing to show up at eight o'clock, stick it out till five, refrain from smoking, and not get in the way.

I was a clerk. I had a small cubicle all my own, I didn't have to be gracious and charming, I didn't have to use that blasted cash register and frighten myself with the bell, and all I had to do was collect little pieces of price tickets that the salesgirls tore off and sort them out by code numbers and add them up.

Everything went along fine. I hardly ever had to use the roller towel, and I might be a clerk in Stern Brothers to this very day if something hadn't happened. The buyer of the house-dress department made a lucky purchase of ten thousand flowered voile dresses that a dress manufacturer had run up by mistake after *he* made a lucky purchase of thirty thousand yards of voile that some voile manufacturer had covered with flowers on one of those gloomy days when everything goes wrong. The day before they were to go on sale at $1.29, the buyer asked me to come in early the next morning and dress all the plaster mannikins in the voile dresses for her.

I, always co-operative, agreed and, as soon as I got to the store, selected a voile dress and started to put it on the figure. I immediately discovered that the dress had no placket anywhere. However, as I pulled it down over the figure, the situation changed rapidly and plackets appeared all over the place. I hastily tucked the dress in a trash bin and tried another, larger voile dress. More plackets.

When the store opened, customers stormed out of the elevators in shock waves, and there I stood, in the thick of it, with three naked mannikins and a trash bin full of flowered voile dresses.

When the buyer arrived she was not absolutely delighted with my arrangements, and my career ground to a halt again.

By this time deep furrows began to appear on my mother's and father's brows, for now they were saddled with this daughter who had that hair, no college degree, a broken nose, no horsemanship, and to top it off was proving to be a schlemihl who couldn't earn a living.

By now my sister had given up a glowing career as a social service worker and was happily married, and there I was, still hanging around the house losing jobs and *not getting any younger.*

They sent me to a teacher to learn to play bridge but I was unable to grasp the fundamentals (let me see, does an ace count as one?) and after the second lesson the teacher took up basket weaving. *I* liked to play chess, but my parents said sternly that chess was *not* a social asset.

My father decided that a really good typist and stenographer could always get a job, so I dutifully went off to secretarial school and promptly on finishing the course got a job addressing envelopes for a map company. I was a very good envelope addresser and it was two weeks before anyone noticed that I was the bottleneck that was licking the envelopes to seal them and sticking three cent stamps neatly in place with the heel of my palm.

It was somewhere along in here that I met this man I spoke of and my business career was gently laid to rest.

My parents were nervous wrecks until the wedding actually took place. My mother was certain that at any moment this reckless character would stop to take a really good look at my hair, while my father was sure that one disastrous day this rash fellow would ask me to join him in a game of tennis or a brisk canter through the park, and the whole thing would be called off.

This man, at the time we were married, *did own a tennis racquet,* which he brought with him as part of his dowry along with a dented trumpet. True, the tennis racquet needed restringing, and it had no press and no case, and he had no tennis balls, but he did have this racquet and as a matter of fact, it is now in the hall closet, covered with sixteen years' accumulation of dust and galoshes.

The first few years we were married, he took the

racquet out every spring and looked at it. "I guess I ought to get out and play some tennis," he'd say, turning the racquet about in his hands and poking exploratory fingers through the holes in the stringing. That was the point at which I was supposed to spring to my feet with glad cries and say, "Yes, let's!" However, as I never spring, I just sat there like a strand of spaghetti and went on reading. "I guess I ought to call somebody up," he'd say next. Then after a while he'd say, "I guess I ought to have my racquet restrung." Then after another while he'd get up and put the racquet back in the closet.

For the past ten years or so he has not removed the racquet from its bed of dust. It is just there, part of the house like a window or a hot air register.

I met this lethargic individual in a corner of a crowded room at a party, and it was love at second sight. At first sight, he decided I was an introverted trained nurse, whereas the girl he had brought with him was an extroverted model named Yvonne. Yvonne had curly hair. Red.

At our second meeting he found out that I really wasn't a trained nurse at all, but the question of how he came to call me up is one that has never been answered to the satisfaction of either of us. It is just one of those puzzling things, like bird migrations. Probably Yvonne had another date. But I don't like to question these things. I just go through life taking the tennis racquets as they come.

When my parents found out that in addition to being a man, willing to marry me, he was sound in wind and limb, and capable of earning a living on and off to boot, it was a great burden off their minds.

How I Acquired My Lack of Poise

Up to my fifth year, I was sublimely unself-conscious, completely and magnificently at home in any surroundings and comfortably friendly with any creature, on two legs or four. There was only one trouble. I was—no matter how they tried to disguise it with dresses that were striped vertically or otherwise cunningly devised—shaped exactly like a butterball. I even moved like a butterball—frontwards, backwards, or sideways, depending on the position I happened to be in when I started.

This condition did not bother *me* in the least. I was quite capable of rolling down a flight of stairs, picking myself up unconcernedly, and continuing whatever conversation had been momentarily interrupted. My social poise was not in the least disturbed by my lack of physical poise. Apparently it *did* bother grownups, however, and eventually it was decided, over my head, that I was to study ballet. Ballet dancing, my parents were convinced, would enable me to go forth in life serene and graceful.

My older sister, who was eight then, was much too tall and thin, and they decided to fix both of us up at once. We took lessons in a class of about thirty little girls, and our teacher's name was something Russian that ended with the syllable -ova. For years after, I had the delusion that I had studied with Pavlova. At that age a few consonants one way or the other don't bother you much.

We were all togged out with little dancing dresses and ballet slippers and wads of lamb's wool for the toes. And since all the dancing dresses were alike, the net result was that right at the very beginning my sister looked even taller and thinner than she had before, with a great deal of long leg sticking out below the hem of her dress like a stork, and I looked more than ever like a butterball—especially since my dress happened to be yellow.

The classroom was a nightmare of long mirrors, and for the first time in my life I saw myself objectively in a group of other children. Since we were all dressed exactly alike, the hideous difference between the way I looked and the way they looked was at once clear to me. The word "butterball" took on a new and terrible meaning.

The dancing didn't go too well, either. I was (and still am, since I avoid exercise in any form) remarkably limber. So limber, in fact, that we might as well admit that I am double-jointed almost all over. Everything wobbles. When all the other children took a position, I tried to do it too, only some joint always gave way and started bending in the other direction. I never did succeed in standing on my toes, but I was quite successful in concealing this fact by standing behind other children who could and often did stand on their toes. If Madame Pastrova (or Varnova) knew it, she never said anything.

At the end of the year there was the recital. Since it

was my first public appearance, I did not yet have the sense to be afraid. It was not until the audience was all assembled and the dancing had started that the full horror of it struck me. I was the smallest of the children, in height if in nothing else, and I had to dance in the very front. I suddenly realized that there I was in front of all those people, and there was *nobody to hide behind.* I stood stock still, while I took the situation in; then I burst into tears and was led quietly away.

There were no more dancing lessons—especially after it was discovered that persistent effort to achieve position number five had flattened my sister's feet and mine. The dancing lessons were replaced for a while with foot exercises designed to repair the damage, and it was a good many years before my feet once more regained a somewhat normal shape. We were further supplied with heavy metal arch supports which caused our shoes to bulge and crack and which caused us to walk with a peculiar thumping gait.

Now that these torments are past, I'm not too unhappy. There doesn't seem to be much opportunity, in my part of society, for breaking into dances, and I'm no longer shaped like an egg anyway, so it isn't any great loss that the lessons were so unfruitful. And now, every time I crash into an end table, I'm just full of poise—I tell the story about the time I took ballet lessons.

My Formal Education

Since the large part of my formal education was obtained in the public schools of New York City, I suppose it was not really unique or extraordinary. Yet as I look back, I do think there must have been something a *little* peculiar about it.

While reading the reviews of the Robeson *Othello*, it suddenly occurred to me that I had never read *Othello* or, for that matter, any Shakespeare to speak of. Shakespeare, as I learned about him in high school, really wasn't much of a writer. He was always committing atrocities, such as mixed metaphors and anachronisms, which were pointed out to us as examples of things *never* to do. The examples which we were taught over and over were (1) the clock's striking, in *Julius Caesar* (the worst sort of anachronism), and (2) "the slings and arrows of outrageous fortune" (a really first-rate example of the dread mixed metaphor). We were forced to memorize the "To be or not to be" speech, but only, I supposed, so that we would remember this terrible confusion of metaphors.

This all started me thinking about the rest of my education, and I decided to try to remember exactly what I did learn in school, being careful to separate it from what I learned by poking around in the children's room at the St. Agnes branch of the Public Library.

In kindergarten I learned to carry a small green chair around, and I learned to cut paper with dull scissors.

In grade school I learned some arithmetic—that is, I picked up some knowledge of addition, subtraction, and multiplication, but I must have been sick when they taught long division. At any rate, I missed it somehow, and I never learned it in school. One day I discovered that all the other children were able to do a mysterious and complicated process with numbers, called "division," and I went home crying. My mother made an attempt to teach it to me, but she put the answer out to the right, and in school they put it above, so I was never convinced that what she was teaching me was the right thing.

I learned to bound Manhattan Island, and I learned to bound the United States, and I learned the names of the continents, and I think there were some principal rivers and principal mountains and principal cities in there too.

I read Dickie Dare and I still remember how it went. "Dickie Dare went to school. On the way he met a cow. 'Good morning, cow,' said Dickie Dare. 'Moo moo,' said the cow." He also met a duck and I suppose some other animals, but I no longer remember them. I read "The Lady or the Tiger" at least twenty times and wrote as many compositions about how I thought it ended. That must have been considered quite the thing for stimulating the little minds in those days. My other work in English consisted in writing compositions entitled "My Vacation," "My Pet," "The Greatest Man in the

World," and so on. One teacher told us that an original and interesting ending for a composition was, "Don't you think so too?" So after that we all ended our compositions with the identical originality and felt quite proud of ourselves.

I learned to parse a sentence, with handsome little diagrams showing how it worked.

I learned to sew, and I got second prize for my graduation dress (although I cheated—I had my mother and my grandmother slaving over the hard parts), but in cooking class all we ever made was cream sauce (but nothing to put the cream sauce on) and once we made gingerbread.

In history I learned several things. I learned that there was something called the American Revolution, and we won because the Hessians got drunk on Christmas Eve. I learned a string of dates which were committed to memory perfectly, but what they were I had no idea. If you gave me the number 1066, out came its correct partner, the Norman Conquest, but who Norman was and who he conquered were mysteries to me. If you told me the number 1588, I would say, quick as anything, "Drake and the Spanish Armada." Drake, to me, was a kind of cake, and as for the Spanish Armada, it never occurred to me that it meant anything at all.

I also learned 1492, 1776, 1789, 1865, 1215, and several others, with the right events. It didn't matter if you didn't know them all, because on the examinations you were given the lists of dates and events and you had to match them up, so you always teamed up the leftover dates with the leftover events and had a pretty fair chance of being right.

I learned music appreciation. This consisted in learning the first two bars of the "Danse Macabre," the "Dance of the Hours," "Rustle of Spring," and "The Swan," and the right names to go with them, so that at examination time we could infallibly write down " 'Rustle of Spring' by Sinding," after the two opening bars were played.

We were also taught with some care to pronounce Saint-Saëns correctly, which was evidently of great importance.

When I was twelve and armed with all this knowledge, I went on to high school. In high school I learned many different things.

I learned to climb a rope ladder and to dance the Highland Fling.

I learned that a bean is either a monocotyledon or a dicotyledon, I no longer remember which, and I learned that the skin of an onion is made up of cells which could be seen if you looked at it through a microscope, but unfortunately I never got to look through a microscope until last year, when I bought one of my own. I learned that most plants will die unless they get water and sun, and we proved this in experiments in which we denied beans water and sun until they died. I learned to draw a grasshopper, and I learned that some part of a carrot is called the cortex, but I don't know which part.

I read some of the *Odyssey*, but that class came after swimming class, so mostly we just dried our hair on the radiators. Somebody forgot to tell us who Homer was and when he lived or in fact anything about him, and nobody ever mentioned that the *Odyssey* had anything to do with Greek literature. Indeed nobody ever mentioned Greece or Rome in my presence all through my entire schooling.

I learned that my voice was denasalized and I intoned "The brown cow browsed around the brown barn" and "The man ran along the sand with his hat in his hand" more times than I care to think about. I don't know if it did any good or not. I learned that the correct way to breathe is not from the chest but from the diaphragm, but I was unable to change my breathing habits and so have continued to breathe in my chest anyway, and I suppose my voice is still denasalized.

I took physics, and I found out that if you heated water long enough it boiled and gave off steam, and I learned how to hook up an electric bell (though when our doorbell goes out of order I have to call the superintendent because I don't know where the wires are, and anyway it looks different from the ones in school). And I learned that if you pick up a hot Bunsen burner, it hurts.

That was all there was to it. Someone in the school system miscalculated the time necessary to learn all these things, and at the end of three years I discovered suddenly that I had passed plenty of Regents' examinations to get into college, but that alas! I could not graduate from high school because I had only had three years of rope climbing and Highland Fling. This led to all sorts of difficulties, but since I had already been admitted to the university to which I had applied, I simply ignored the difficulties.

At college I learned interpretive dancing (in a short, loose green garment) and I was forced to play tennis until a certain date, regardless of the weather. I learned that if you play tennis in the snow in a raccoon coat, it is not good for the racquet.

I learned that El Greco was a madman, Picasso worse, and that Leonardo's "Last Supper" has flaked off considerably because he was so stupid about experimenting with new media.

I wrote daily compositions (only they were called themes at college) and they were all carefully corrected for punctuation. They were always entitled "On" something, and I no longer ended them with a question necessarily, since that was not required in college.

I learned that if you have steam under pressure and you let it go through a rubber tube that is slightly rotted, the tube will burst and the steam will escape quickly and scald whoever happens to get in the way. I found out that you have to take the whole science of physics on faith, because no demonstration in the lecture hall ever turns out the way it's supposed to, and that furthermore the experiments don't turn out any better in the laboratory. Especially when your lab partner is a fluffy blonde who leans over your shoulder at the crucial moment and dips pale blue ribbons and bits of lace ruffle in your crucible. I learned that there are very few nerve endings on the skin of the back of your hand, that you can see better in the daytime than at night, and that if you drop a baby he doesn't like it.

I learned how to find the volume of a truncated pyramid, but I've not used this knowledge lately.

I learned, when I came home after two years, that in the public library they have the most amazing books— all about animals, and psychoanalysis, and fungi, and Greece, and languages, and insects, and Rome, and parasites, and China, and music, and semantics, and India, and revolutions, and spiders, and people, and amoebae, and Persian painting, and fishes, and dead languages, and Toltec sculpture.

I think books are wonderful. Don't you think so too?

Lend Me Your Ear, Roman

I never got around to studying Latin. I had an older sister who did, and when I listened to her piteous moans while she memorized nouns of the third declension, I determined never to let that happen to me. However, recently it occurred to me that I didn't know what "E Pluribus Unum" meant, or even "Tempus Fugit," or "Carpe Diem," or anything. I decided therefore, at my advanced age, to remedy the situation, purchased a first-year Latin Grammar, and set to work. I memorize declensions while stirring lumps in the gravy, conjugate verbs while pouring too much bleach in the washing machine, and carry on enchanting little conversations with myself while the bacon burns.

I have finished the first seven lessons, and I feel ready now to converse charmingly and display my hard-won knowledge, but so far nobody has given me the right conversational cue. People around here don't seem to talk much about what the troops of Galba are doing to the walled towns of the Germans. I've been waiting and waiting for someone to come up to me on the street and say, "By the way, what are the troops of Galba doing to the walled towns of the Germans?" And then, without hardly even thinking, I will reply graciously, in faultless Latin, "Copiae Galbae, amici Gallorum, oppida Germanorum oppugnant." In case you happen to be suspicious that I really don't know what it means, I can now translate brilliantly, and without a moment's hesitation, "The troops of Galba, friends of the Gauls, attack the walled towns of the Germans." I could then add, casually, "Incolae insularum copias Galbae laudant."

Unfortunately someone did come up to me on the street the other day and said, "Caesar vadum hujus fluminis temptare parat," and all I could say was, "He *did?*" That's in Lesson Twenty-three, or, as we Romans say, in Lesson XXIII.

Here I am now, getting on to nouns of the third declension, and I'll be able to say really interesting sentences about rowers and stones and embankments, and I haven't had a chance to show off *yet.*

Meanwhile, all the closets need cleaning, and there isn't a thing in the house for dinner, and I still haven't found out what "E Pluribus Unum" means.

Oh well, tempus fugit, as we educated people offhandedly remark, and I'd better carpe diem and get to work.

Camera Very Obscura!

I have a Brownie Reflex camera purchased in nineteen thirty-nine for three dollars and ninety-five cents. It has taken lots of pictures. In fact, the only time it ever *hasn't* taken a picture was once when I had my thumb in front of the lens. It has taken close-ups (portrait attachment, $1.95) and long shots. It has operated in sun, cloud, hurricane, blizzard, and indoors (flash attachment, $6.95). I even tried a couple of fancy still lifes, and it obligingly took those, only the composition wasn't very good. It takes black-and-white pictures just fine, and it takes color pictures very satisfyingly.

I love that camera. Of course I readily acknowledge that I am not a camera fan. I just like to take pictures of things and stick them in albums so that twenty years later we can look at them and say how funny we looked. My standards are not high.

I could get along perfectly nicely this way for the rest of my life. I don't need light meters or tape measures or even very much patience. I just need that little box, a modicum of light, and a couple of children. But our friends and relatives don't like it. "Why don't you get yourself a *real* camera," they say with disgust.

This I could ignore, but our friends can't. "Here," they say kindly, "you borrow our camera for one week and just *try* it." It seems everybody but me has a *really*

44

good camera, and we've had all kinds of Leicas, Graflexes, and Zeisses palmed off on us this way. At the beginning I used to take the camera for a week and make a real effort, but I never could get any pictures. All that happened was that while I was struggling with apertures and shutter speeds, I was wasting good film and failing to get priceless pictures of things I really *needed* like the children digging for treasure under our only decent shrub. Each time I would return the camera, thanking the friend politely, and humbly apologizing for my failure. But I couldn't make them understand that I didn't care about the quality of the pictures, and their feelings were always hurt.

The trouble may be that when I was a child, my father always used to take pictures of my sister and me with a *really good* camera, and it was an event absolutely to be dreaded and fought against with every bit of strength in our little muscles. It involved endless preparations with speculation about the quality of the light, measurements with tape measures, experimenting with different positions to improve the background and composition while I fought off sunstroke. At the end, he had absolutely marvelous pictures, sharp, clear, and beautifully composed, of my sister and me scowling horribly and squinting in the sunlight.

Lately the situation has been worsening. There's been so much talk around here about depth of focus and shutter speed that I've got so confused I can hardly load my little Brownie any more. I wish everybody would go somewhere and leave me alone long enough to take some more blurry pictures of my little boys with bits of washline fluttering in the background. Chee!

The Rebel

My mother worked awfully hard to teach me politeness, courtesy, and common everyday good manners. "Always say 'thank you,'" she told me, "and 'please.' Don't tread on people's toes and don't jostle old ladies. Keep your elbows in when you cut your meat and don't toy with the silverware. Never blow bubbles in your milk and don't make comments about the food. Always modulate your voice, don't point, and never make personal remarks. Consider others before you speak or act."

I have tried to behave nicely, but I find now that it was a total waste of time. Wherever I turn, no matter how much I modulate my voice, keep my elbows in, and refrain from blowing bubbles in my milk, I seem to arouse wrath and antagonism on every side.

When I get on a bus, if I hand the driver a quarter and ask him politely for change (keeping my voice nicely modulated and remembering to say "please"), he turns on me and shouts, "What's da matter around here? Don't nobody never have da right change?" He then proceeds to curse me roundly, not quite under his breath, while I cringe and creep to the back of the bus to lick my wounds.

Sometimes the bus is crowded up front, and there's plenty of room at the back, but a large, elderly woman is in the way. My mother told me never to jostle old ladies, so I try to squeeze gently past, but the elderly lady is made of too too solid flesh, and not even an eel could get by. The bus driver stops the bus, turns around, looks directly at me, and yells, "Fa Crise sake, step to da back of da bus, will ya?" I try once again to squeeze past the elderly lady, and she turns on me, glares, and starts to mutter, "Well, I must say, young people nowadays—" Everybody is mad at *me*.

I go out in the morning and ring for the elevator. It does not come. I remember my mother's warning, "Always consider others before you speak or act." Perhaps, I think, the elevator man is busy delivering a package, and he will come soon. I wait. Meanwhile someone on the floor below rings for the elevator by simply pressing his finger on the button and keeping it there. Presently the elevator arrives at my floor. I step in. The elevator man turns his face away from me and mutters angrily, "Ring, ring, ring! For God's sake, what do they think I am, anyway?" He thinks *I* did it.

When I go to a restaurant for dinner, after I have ordered my meal, I usually ask the waiter to bring my coffee with my main course. I always remember to say "please," and I keep my hands folded in my lap, but no matter—he acts as though I had just attacked him with a meat cleaver. He casts his eyes up to the ceiling, flings up his hands in a gesture of utter despair of the foibles of humanity at large and me in particular, and goes off shaking his head with disgust and quietly emitting oaths. I cannot understand why it should be so much harder to bring the coffee with the main course than it is to bring it with the dessert. All I can make of it is

47

that there are things my mother didn't teach me.

Occasionally I stop at a newsstand to buy a magazine. I stand there as my mother taught me, head up, chin in, gloves pulled on nice and smooth, the hem of my dress even, and my stocking seams straight, and I ask pleasantly, "Do you have a copy of such-and-such a magazine, please?" The news dealer wheels around, rage in his eye, like a dog that has just been deprived of a bone. "It's all sold out," he yells out of the side of his mouth. "Sold out this morning," he shouts, as though it were a calamity equal in horror to the bubonic plague and all my fault. He turns back to his stand, muttering. "What do they think anyway," he says, "I got nuttin' to do all day but save old magazines?" He looks as though he were muttering to the piles of newspapers, but I know who he's mad at, all right. It's *me!*

One day I needed a pair of shoes, and accordingly went to a shoe store. A salesman came over. "What do you want?" he said. "I'd like a pair of black shoes, please," I said. He stared at me as though I had just murdered his wife and five small children. "What size?" he asked. "Seven-and-a-half, please," I said nicely, the way my mother taught me. His face flushed with rage. "Seven and a half!" he shouted, baring his teeth. "We don't have any shoes in size seven and a half," he yelled in disgust. If I'd asked for size seven, or even size eight, his tone implied, he might have had some shoes, but *I* had to walk in and waste his time asking for size seven *and a half!*

I don't like to suggest that my mother's advice wasn't the best, but—from now on I'm going to blow bubbles in my milk whenever I feel like it.

48

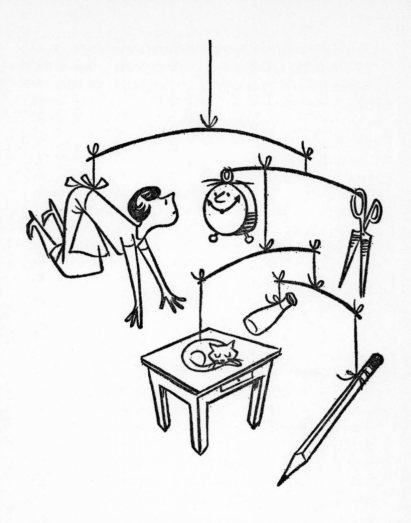

Domestic Definitions

The Kitchen Table

A kitchen table is an oblong piece of wood that rests on four long thin pieces of wood and is often found in the middle of the kitchen with a cat sitting on it.

It is a piece of furniture intended for use as a place to prepare or serve food.

It is the cat's bed. The cat has a much better bed on the floor not three feet away from the table, but she doesn't like that bed because she can't see out the window from it. Besides, if she lies in that one, she can't get cat hairs in the sugar bowl.

The legs of the table are the cat's scratching posts. There is a cat scratching post in the corner, but the legs of the table are better because they're so handy to the bed.

The kitchen table is also the place where you dump your raincoat. Of course there is a closet in the hall, but that's too far from the Coca-Cola.

The kitchen table is where* you build model ships, crystal radio sets, telescopes, etc. Of course there is a fully equipped workshop in the basement, with bench, lathe, drill press, electric sander, power saw, and overhead lights. But it's so *untidy* down there.

---

*My public school grammar teacher said you must *never* say a noun is where. But I don't care. I say it all the time.

The kitchen table is the place to clean the fish tank. *Anyone* knows *that*.

The kitchen table is the family stepladder for changing light bulbs in ceiling fixtures, and it is also what you lay out the wallpaper on when wallpapering, and it is where you lay out the material when sewing, and it is also where you dump the logs for the fireplace after you have come panting up the cellar stairs desperate for a resting place.

Don't know where to put your galoshes? Can't find a place to clean the bird cage? Splice home movies? De-flea the cat? Manicure your nails? Polish shoes? Store your collection of bugs, worms, and caterpillars? Investigate the properties of vinegar and baking soda? Chop firewood? Pitch a tent? Why don't you come and use my kitchen table? Everybody else does.

The Milk Bottle

The milk bottle is a strong glass container of exactly one quart liquid capacity and generally contains, of all things, milk. It is a very useful object. If there were no milk bottles, when the milkman brought the milk in the morning it would just lie there and spread itself out all over the kitchen floor. This would be very insanitary as no matter how clean you keep your kitchen floor, the milkman himself has just stepped all over it, tracking in dirt and leaves and mud. And the milk, besides now being very dirty and probably not fit to drink, would be very hard to pick up and put in the icebox.

The milk bottle is a handy place to leave notes for the milkman asking him to leave three quarts of milk and a dozen eggs. (Maybe you'd rather leave him a note asking for one quart of milk and a pound of butter. *I* don't know what you need. You'll just have to look in the refrigerator yourself.)

The milk bottle, when empty, is always at hand ready for use. When the fish tank needs cleaning, the milk bottle stands by to be used as a temporary fish home.

The milk bottle is the best equipment known for all kinds of scientific experiments with hard-boiled eggs and burning paper, or bicarbonate of soda and vinegar, and it is just grand for filling with water and holding upside down with a piece of paper over the neck to demonstrate the force of air pressure. You can also fill it with water, put the head of a match in it, and cork it. This makes a diver that goes up and down when you press on the cork.

The milk bottle is an excellent vessel for storing *all kinds of things* in the refrigerator. Many people mistakenly believe it to be suitable only for milk because of its being inappropriately called a milk bottle. Actually it can serve equally well for storing leftover chicken soup or fruit juice or martinis. You *could* put in chocolate pudding or hamburgers but they would be very hard to get out.

Milk bottles make excellent doorstops, and can be used in an emergency to hold up a window with a broken sash cord. These are summertime uses. In the winter they are excellent vessels for filling with water and leaving outside on the window sill to see how high the ice comes over the top for demonstrating the expansion of water when it freezes. (Have you ever read *anything* so absolutely scientific as this article?)

Milk bottles have many uses. They are man's friend.

Clocks

A clock is a round thing with two hands that tells you when you're too late. When you're in a hurry, it speeds up. When you have time to kill, it slows down. This is very annoying of it.

Some clocks go too fast, in which case you are always standing around uneasily waiting for people. Some clocks go too slow, and then other people stand around getting mad at you.

There is no such thing as a dependable clock. The ones that have to be wound up by hand often stop because you forget, and the ones that go by electricity stop during the night when you least suspect it because there was a storm and a power failure. Sometimes they stop because somebody blew a fuse. (I *told* somebody not to plug in that heater while the toaster was on.) You're far better off going by the sun which is a good deal less likely to go wrong and hardly likely at all to stop.

People didn't always have this mania for clocks and keeping track of minutes. People didn't even always have clocks. When two Romans made a date, they just said, "See you Tuesday afternoon at the barber's." Then everybody could take it easy. It didn't matter if they got there at two o'clock or three o'clock or four o'clock. If it was between noon and sundown, they were right on time. In some countries today everybody has clocks, but nobody pays any attention to them. "Nine o'clock" means anything from nine-thirty to twelve.

I have a clock that tells the hour, minute, second, day, and date, but it is extremely unreliable as it only works for months having thirty-one days. This means that at least six times a year you have to remember to reset the date, and if you should forget, the clock is off not by minutes, but by days, sometimes even years. This is nerve wracking. You have to consult a regular calendar daily in order to be sure it isn't time to reset the calendar clock.

Some clocks have chimes, so you can know the hour without even bothering to look up. This is very fine and even sounds quite pleasant, but if you should forget to wind up the chime while unfortunately remembering to wind up the clockworks, terrible things happen. It chimes three at midnight, and this is disconcerting just as you're falling asleep. Then you have to take a sleeping pill, and then it's hard to wake up on time the next morning, and you're likely to throw your whole week off schedule.

Some clocks, both electric and hand-powered, have alarms. The more pleasant the sound of the alarm, the more horrible it is, as it fools you for a minute in your sleep into thinking it is something not really horrible. The shock, when you realize that it is, after all, an alarm, is even worse than just a plain horrible shock in the first place that jolts you out of your comforting dream with a start and a tremble. It is a curious thing that alarm clocks never wake the other members of a family. No matter how hideous the clamor, it only wakes this member of the family. Everybody else sleeps happily on, unaware of the terrible little struggle that is going on, with cigarette packages falling down, telephones crashing, ash trays spilling in the cold and dark of early morning as you fumble and grope for the little switch that turns off the gruesome clanging.

At least water clocks, marked candles, hourglasses and sundials made hardly any noise at all. What makes us think we're so smart?

Excuse me please. I think my electric calendar clock may be a day or two off again.

Scissors

A pair of scissors is two long pieces of metal hitched together in the middle with loops at one end. Nobody has ever found out whether they—or it—are singular or plural. You put a thumb and a forefinger (preferably on the same hand) through the loops and squeeze. Cutting may result.

There are many kinds of scissors such as manicure scissors, sewing scissors, paper shears, wire cutters, tin snips, hedge shears, etc. You are not supposed to mix them up. However, in most homes, the manicure scissors are customarily used to cut wire, the sewing scissors to cut nails, etc. I don't know why this is so, unless it's because scissors move *about* so. No matter how carefully you put the sewing scissors in the sewing box, the next time you look for them, they turn up in the garage, while the hedge shears have now disappeared and turn up in the cellar, and the pinking shears suddenly appear in the kitchen drawer, all ready for cutting up parsley. Oh well. They all *cut* really, so what's the difference?

The real trouble is when they don't appear at all, and this is a frequent occurrence. All eight of them suddenly and mysteriously vanish, leaving you to struggle with a paring knife or a coping saw, and you can't cut cloth with *them*. However, sooner or later some or all of the scissors are bound to turn up again, often in one of the children's beds or on the cellar steps or behind the stove.

In the absence of a hammer (and it generally is) scissors can be used to remove nails and tacks, while in the absence of a punch, one point of the scissors will serve nicely to make a new hole in a belt or shoe strap. When a point breaks off, scissors can do very well as a screwdriver.

Scissors can be sharpened, but I have never seen a true case of it. People have umbrellas mended, knives sharpened, skates sharpened, lawn mowers sharpened and cars tuned up, but scissors are left to chew as best they can. Perhaps it's because at the moment the knife-grinder appears, the scissors have all disappeared again. Well, what's the difference? When they get *really* dull, put them back in mother's sewing box.

Pencils

A pencil is an instrument for writing. It is delicious to chew, with its crisp outside and tender inside, and its lovely aroma of crushed wood.

A pencil does not suddenly run out of ink smack in the middle of a word, and it does not leak on your fingers. It does not get puzzling little hairs caught in its point, nor does it ever catch crabs and spatter. Except for the typewriter, the pencil is the ultimate achievement today in writing utensils. It doesn't even cost anything, practically.

The pencil can be dropped without fear. It does not break easily, and should the point snap, it can be sharpened as good as new in a second. It is light in weight and can be stuck handily behind the ear (should you chance to be a grocery-store clerk) or in the hair (should you happen to be a lady clerk with long hair). It can be carried with impunity in airplanes at high altitudes. It will write under water. It will also write under beer, coffee, and Seven-Up.

The pencil is an excellent lever and can be used to pry up stuck windows, open stuck bureau drawers, stuck jar tops, stuck paint cans, etc. In fact, anything that's stuck can be pried with a pencil. Of course the pencil often breaks, but then, *sometimes* it doesn't.

The pencil can serve, in a pinch, as a bookmark (though this is not particularly good for the book) and as a paint stirrer, especially the eraser end.

Should you ever want to punch holes in soap, there is no finer implement than the point end of a pencil. (*I* don't know why you should want to punch holes in soap. That's your affair.)

Anything that you need a screwdriver for (except driving screws), only you can never find a screwdriver when you need one, you can use a pencil for. You can always find a pencil. (Unless you need one for writing— then it's the screwdriver that turns up.)

When you catch insects in a Mason jar and you put aluminum foil over the top, the pencil is what you use to punch the air holes, and when you lose a needle in the crack between the floor boards, what do you use to get it out? Say, you *are* quick.

After you've cut yourself with the screwdriver, you use the pencil to make the tourniquet, and you also poke the pencil through the hole of the sardine-can key for leverage.

Pencils are very life-enhancing.

I Married a Bibliomaniac

But I'm *All Right*

I've been married for seventeen years but until now I've had no way of knowing if I'm happy or not. I've been haunted by the thought that all these years I may have been married to the wrong man.

Now, however, my doubts are all dispelled, for the other day I found in a magazine a little questionnaire for wives, intended to help them decide this very thing. It said,

"Does your husband:
1. Smoke excessively?
2. Use extreme unforgivable profanity?
3. Gamble, or take serious financial risks?
4. Blame you for everything that goes wrong?
5. Try to prevent you from having friends?
6. Keep you upset and uneasy much of the time?
7. Have an ungovernable temper?
8. Ridicule your standards and ideals?
9. Lack acceptable table manners?
10. Belittle you in public?
11. Compare you unfavorably with other wives?
12. Spend too much on himself?
13. Have crude or vulgar habits?
14. Treat you rudely and disrespectfully?"

Needless to say, in the ideal marriage, the wife could

happily answer "no" to every question. Three or more "yesses" indicate trouble. In my case, the answer is "yes" to all fourteen. Here, let me take them one at a time.

Smoke excessively? That man smokes from the minute his eyes are open in the morning till he closes them at night. Sometimes he even wakes up during the night to cram in an extra cigarette. Smoke, smoke, smoke. Between meals, during meals, while he's shaving, indoors, outdoors. Everywhere he goes, he strews cigarette butts. The ash trays are full, and the worst of it is that half the time when he puts his cigarettes out, he doesn't put them *out*. Sometimes I think he smokes as much as I do. He's disgusting.

Use unforgivable profanity? You should just *hear* him. The other day when one of the children dropped a hot soldering iron on his foot, I could clearly hear him say, "Darn!" all the way upstairs. He's awful.

Gamble, or take serious financial risks? Gamble is hardly the word for it. That man is a free-lance writer and has supported this family, man, woman, and two children, in this careless, reckless way for seventeen years. Our whole existence is predicated on financial risks. Laws-a-mercy, we never know where our next meal is coming from. One year our whole income tax was eight dollars, and the next year it took two Brink's trucks to carry it to the Office of Internal Revenue.

Blame me for everything that goes wrong? Well I should say he does. Take that time when I drove the car through the side of the garage and smashed a headlight and crumpled a fender and wrecked the garage door. He blamed me for *that*. Or take the time I left the water running in the kitchen sink while I went out to buy some Good Humors and I just happened to meet a neighbor and we just happened to get to chatting a little, and when I got back the whole kitchen floor had to be torn up and a new one installed. He blamed me for *that*. Or the time I dropped a whole pot roast on his new pants. He blamed me for *that*. I tell you, that man blames me for every little thing. It's terrible.

Try to prevent me from having friends? Well I'm here to tell you. He stands in the doorway and dares people to cross the threshold. "Don't you try to make friends with *her*," he tells them, "I work at home and I need peace and quiet."

Keep me upset and uneasy much of the time? *All* the time. Every time he buys me a new fur coat or a new watch, or a record I wanted, or offers to do the dishes for me, I'm so uneasy I can hardly sleep or eat. What is he up to *now*, I keep wondering.

Have an ungovernable temper? The least thing makes him fly off the handle. One Halloween night when some boys were having a little fun with their childish pranks, and threw a rock through the window and it grazed his head as well as smashing a storm window and a window, you should have seen him. He was *furious*. And his head only bled a *little*. Boy, does he have a temper.

Ridicule my standards and ideals? He made fun of me just the other day because I wanted to send the telephone company a check for ten cents to cover the dime that was accidentally returned to me in a phone booth. He's *dishonest*.

Lack acceptable table manners? You should see him. He mops up gravy with a piece of bread, he dunks doughnuts, he leans his elbows on the table, he blows on his soup, he stirs his coffee vigorously and if it slops in the saucer he pours it back in the cup. We might as well eat from a *trough*.

Belittle me in public? Public *and* private. "Here," he says, "let me carry that for you. It's too heavy for you." Or, "I'll move the piano, don't you touch it." Or, "I'll build the fire." You'd think I was a child or an invalid.

Compare me unfavorably with other wives? I'll say he does. He compares me unfavorably with the wives of Arthur Miller, for instance, Artie Shaw, Harry James—lots of them.

Spend too much money on himself? There's no end to that man's selfishness. Just last year he bought himself a new raincoat, and the old one was *perfectly good*. It just leaked a little. Last week he bought himself a new pair of eyeglasses for thirty dollars. He could have just squinted a little. He'd have seen, all right. But no. Just selfish. And just because the old car got stuck on the parkway a few times while I was alone in it, he went out and bought a brand new car. When it comes to his own pleasures, he doesn't care *how* he flings money around.

Have crude or vulgar habits? Well! I hate to say it, but sometimes he's positively embarrassing. He bites hangnails, he picks bits of tobacco off his tongue, he slouches in his chair, he scratches his head when he's thinking, he adds up the check before he pays it in a restaurant, if he helps to clear the table he stacks the dishes, he whittles in the living room and he whittles on the front porch steps, and besides, he whistles on the street. Ugh!

Treat me rudely and disrespectfully? Well, he has certainly never put his cloak on a mud puddle for me. All he does is say, "Here, jump." He and the children call me the old witch, and *I don't think that's nice.*

Besides that's not all. There are a few things they forgot on that questionnaire. He plays the hi-fi so hi-fi that I have bruises where the sound waves hit me, he's getting a bald spot on top, his dentist bills are too high, he insists on wearing wool socks that have to be washed carefully, and he throws away perfectly good shoes just because they hurt.

So now I know. There is no doubt whatever that I've been married to the wrong man for seventeen years. The only lucky part of the whole thing is that there was no questionnaire for husbands in that magazine.

The Carpenter Said Nothing but "The Butter's Spread Too Thick"

Sometimes I think of my husband simply as a great, bottomless maw, which it is my Herculean task to keep filled.

Like most human beings, he eats three meals a day. Unfortunately he works at home, so the responsibility for feeding him rests completely on me. Occasionally I am able to coerce him into going out to a drugstore for lunch, but for the most part I have to feed him day in and day out, three times a day, nor does any earthquake, flood, or tempest get me out of it. The three meals a day I would not mind. It is the sad, plaintive look that I get between meals, accompanied by the pathetically pleading eyes and the simple sentence, "I'm hungry," that gets me down.

He's so helpless. Left to himself, with a kitchen stocked with food, he would starve. For ten years the bread has always been in the breadbox, the butter in the icebox, the jam on the second shelf of the cupboard, and so on. But he has never yet been able to find them. I think he tries—he says he does—yet invariably if he goes in search of food, in a few minutes I hear desperate cries from the kitchen. He can't find the jam. There isn't any cream cheese. We've run out of bread. The milk is gone. When I get there, there they are, right where they've always been. We've both found it easier in the long run just to let me do all the fixing and preparing of food in our house. As soon as I hear the sad sentence, "I'm hungry," I go to the kitchen, and without more talk, I whip together some sandwiches, milk, fruit, and cookies in the vain but eternal hope that it will keep him going till dinner. I want to be fair, though, so in all truthfulness I must admit that on two occasions he was able to get himself a glass of milk and some chocolate crackers all by himself.

Now not only does he get hungry, though this in itself is bad enough, considering how often he does it, but he gets hungry for special things. Or rather, specially *not* for certain things.

"I'm hungry," he'll say, for the millionth time, "what is there to eat?" He knows perfectly well what there is to eat, having been eating it for years, but still he asks, in all sincerity, "What is there to eat?" I go through the list patiently. There's milk, coffee, tea, chocolate, tomato juice, orange juice, Coca-Cola, cream soda, and ginger ale. There's bread, cake, cookies, crackers. There's butter, cream cheese, jam, jelly, Edam, Camembert, Cheddar. There's fruit, fresh or stewed. There are eggs. There's lettuce, tomatoes, bacon. There's leftover cold beef or chicken, there are cans of tuna and salmon. He listens with deep attention. He thinks for a moment. Then he says, "I don't feel like anything like that. What else is there?" And all the time he manages to look so helpless, so pathetic, like a soft young puppy that's been taken too soon from the warmth of his mother. I'm taken in by it every time, and I launch into a list of the things I could make. I could make pancakes, omelets, waffles, soufflés, or a salad. No, he doesn't feel like anything like that, either. I suggest cereal. Corn Flakes, oatmeal, Cream of Wheat, Rice Krispies, Grape Nuts. . . . No, that isn't quite what he wants either.

He finally compromises, out of sheer hunger (though mind you, he's had, not two hours before, a big meal which he finished with a sigh of repletion and the happy words, "I'm full"), for some saltines spread with butter, cream cheese, and jelly, and several glasses of milk, and perhaps a few pieces of fruit, and maybe a bit of chocolate cake. He sits there eating it, with the food spread out in front of him on the table, and his big sad eyes look just as big and sad when he gets through with it as when he started. He confesses that what he really wanted was a sturgeon sandwich (though the saltine box is quite empty by then, as is the cream cheese package, the jelly glass, the milk bottle, etc.,) and I sit there meditating on the debris and looking at those sad brown eyes, and feeling guiltier and guiltier at having had such a poor assortment of food to offer a hungry man.

I often suspect him of pretending to a helplessness in the kitchen out of laziness. Yet I am forced to believe that it is genuine, for once when I returned home after several weeks in the hospital, he immediately became very sick. When questioned by the doctor, he confessed that he had lived on scrambled eggs the whole time. "They're the easiest thing to fix," he explained.

It is curious though, that although all of our household equipment is always in perfect working order, if I should have to stay in bed for a day with a bad cold and he tries to make breakfast, it suddenly and perversely develops that nothing is working. The percolator won't perk, the toaster won't toast, all the frying pans have miraculously disappeared overnight, and the coffee has suddenly and unaccountably become rancid. In spite of these handicaps, he makes a sustained and heroic effort and staggers from the kitchen after an hour or two, panting and covered with perspiration, triumphantly bearing a tray on which there languishes a cup of evil-looking pale brown liquid, a piece of dry toast, and two hideously mangled eggs. There is no napkin, no spoon, no cream or sugar, salt or pepper or fork. "I don't know how you do it," he says, "fixing all those meals with such very inferior equipment." If, later in the day, I sneak out of bed to go and fix myself a decent cup of coffee, I find enough food smeared over the kitchen for three more breakfasts—mute evidence of a hideous struggle —and there is a trail, from my bed to the kitchen, of the things that were missing from the tray.

As his appetite continues to be in inverse ratio to his

skills in the kitchen, and as his skill at locating a butter knife does not seem to be improving, I see little hope for any rest for me from the ceaseless toil of trying to keep that man filled with food. The worst of it is that through it all, six meals a day, year in, year out, he has not gained an ounce.

He suffers, but he manages to keep a sweet disposition, though mine sometimes wears a little thin. Often, when I'm preparing the sixth meal of the day and feeling guilty because all I have to offer him is smoked salmon or roast lamb when what he really wants is a bit of shad roe, I feel that I can't stand it another minute, and if he didn't have those sad brown eyes, I probably wouldn't.

I Married a Bibliomaniac

I married a bibliomaniac.

Of course I didn't know it at the time. When I first met my husband, he seemed to be a quite normal young man with no very noticeable aberrations. And even after we were married and moved into our first apartment, I didn't notice anything except that he had rather more books than I did, and that he was considerably more concerned with the purchase of bookcases than of nonessentials like chairs and tables.

Our first home was a three-room apartment, with

rooms of a quite decent size, and at the beginning we were very comfortable there. We had four large bookcases in the living room, two smaller ones in the bedroom, and one wide doorway in which we had shelves built. When all the bookcases and shelves were filled, we simply started a second layer. That is, each shelf then contained a row of books behind the row of books that showed. After that we filled in the spaces in each shelf on top of the books with books on their sides.

I still wasn't worried. We bought six sets of bookends and started a row on top of each bookcase. When all the tops were filled, I was slightly troubled, but we just went on to cover the tops of the bureaus, night tables, the desk, and the coffee table with tall piles. The mirror above my bureau disappeared altogether, as did all our pictures. It was then that I somehow thought that he might start to sell a few, but he seemed to consider our apartment as just so many cubic feet of space which he was bound to fill with books.

When every piece of furniture with a flat top was covered, he started on the radiators and the window sills, and when those were all covered, the books simply started growing up in tall wobbly piles from the floor, like stalagmites.

Each chair in the living room had its pile of books towering behind it. As he finished reading a book, he would simply reach behind the chair and lay it on top of the stack.

But perhaps you don't know how a bibliomaniac does his foul work. You see, he doesn't read books like you and me. He is avid for books, and with mountains of books around him, fears that he may at some dreadful moment be left with no book to read, even with the public library just around the corner. Like an alcoholic who can't take a drink unless he has the bottle in front of him, the bibliomaniac can't read a book without a comfortable reserve pile of six more on the arm of his chair.

You may well ask where the books came from. I used to ask too, at the beginning. Now I know only too well. They come from bookstores, rental libraries, public libraries, friends' libraries, secondhand bookstores, by mail from out-of-town bookshops. He studies secondhand bookstores. If a friend mentions a book he's been looking for but has been unable to find, my husband knows. "Go to Blank's," he'll say, "and on the right-hand side of the store, near the window, on the third shelf from the top and about eight books in from the left, you'll find it. It's marked a dollar and a quarter and that's a good price because it's in good condition except for one torn page near the end. Blink's is asking one seventy-five for one in not nearly as good condition." Usually he offers to pick it up for the friend as he would be in the store himself anyway the next day. When we lived in New York he made the rounds of the secondhand bookstores at least once a day except in really bad weather.

You may well ask where the money for the books comes from. I used to wonder, too. Well, I'll tell you, friend. It's simple really. It comes out of the housekeeping money, the clothing money, the vacation money, the furniture money, the theater and movie money, the doctor and dentist money, and any other money that happens to be around. Any money that comes in goes right out again and comes right back in again in a more bulky form—more books. I tell you if I were a silverfish I'd be a happy woman.

When the apartment became so filled with books that our living room had one narrow aisle between the piles through which you could pick your way to the bedroom (if you went sideways), even my husband became dismayed. "I'm going to sell some of these books," he announced one day. "This is ridiculous." Hope rose in my breast as he started shuffling through the books and picking out those that he thought we could bear to sell. He called in a secondhand book dealer and sold enough books, at ten cents a book, to make a nice wide aisle through the living room. But the new space seemed only to give impetus to the book buying, and not only that, but as he roamed the bookshops he kept finding special bargains—books he *really wanted* and at marvelously low prices. Until I showed him his own name in his own handwriting inside the covers of the fresh lot he had just picked up by great good luck, he never knew he had bought back all his own books at forty-nine cents a copy.

My husband has his own code of ethics about books from which he never deviates. It has two rules of conduct: (1) When you borrow a book, never return it unasked. If the people who lent it want it back badly enough, they'll ask for it. If they don't, they probably don't care about it. Besides, they don't love it as much as you do, so they really don't deserve to have it and it's rightfully yours. (2) Never, never, never under any circumstances lend anyone a book. They might not return it.

In the course of time we were blessed with two children and acquired a house in the suburbs. Instead of buying a six or seven room house like ordinary people, we naturally had to take into consideration my husband's affliction, and we bought a great big old house with ten rooms, an attic, a cellar, dozens of closets and cupboards, hallways, and lots of little odd spaces here and there where you could always tuck in an extra bookcase.

It took one whole moving van and one whole day just to move the books, but when we got them in, there was room left over. "There," I thought, "now I'm going to buy a dustcloth and dust the tops of my furniture like other women."

For one mad glorious month I dusted. Then bit by bit, bureau by bureau, table by table, we began to be buried again. The attic got filled up, the extra rooms got filled up, the bedroom got filled up, and now the living room is starting to go. I still have the dining room and the kitchen though, but last week when he hung a shelf in the kitchen for me I thought I saw a light in his eye that didn't belong there.

I only pray that we'll continue to be able to get in and out till the boys are grown. All our doors open in though, so I don't know.

An Oliver, All Right, but a Blickensderfer?

In our house there are four people. Of the four, only two are adults, and of the two adults, both of whom are writers, only one knows how to type. Nevertheless we own one Royal standard (with elite type), one Royal standard (with pica type), one Remington portable, one Oliver, and one Blickensderfer. It's hard to tell whether the Oliver and the Blickensderfer are portable or standard. The two Royals and the Remington are just sort of *there,* sitting on desks, and if anything goes wrong with them or if they need cleaning, they are attended to by perfect strangers who come in from the Royal or Remington companies. The Oliver and the Blickensderfer, however, are tended personally by my husband. They have been cleaned, polished, rubbed, aligned, oiled, and loved, and the golden oak case for the Blickensderfer has been sanded and polished till it gleams as it did the day it left its factory. Unfortunately, although the Blickensderfer is in absolutely perfect condition, the Oliver has lost its I. My husband searched, for two years, for an I type bar for an Oliver, but stores just don't seem to keep stocks of I type bars for Olivers any more. This has been a bitter disappointment, and only the acquisition of the perfect Blickensderfer has helped to alleviate the pain.

I know how much the Oliver cost, because my husband made the mistake of paying for it by check, and I'm the poor slob who has to balance the checkbook every month. (The reason I have to balance the checkbook is that my husband won't do it on the grounds that banks don't make mistakes and that it's a silly waste of time. He makes this assertion in spite of the fact that we once were the victims of a professional forger, three times have been the victims of mixups with some other people named Smith, and once were the victims of a plain old arithmetic mistake on the part of the bank.) I also know how much the Moxie sign on our kitchen wall cost, and I know how much he paid for the Model A Ford convertible, but since those days he has learned to pay for things with cash, so I don't know how much the Blickensderfer cost. We're probably both happier this way, and my gastritis has improved a lot.

I keep wondering if the Blickensderfer might perhaps be a legitimate business-expense tax deduction when we get around to filing our 1958 return. Of course it probably won't, because he won't talk to our accountant because accountants are so *fussy*, and I can't tell the accountant how much it cost because he won't tell *me*, so there we are, with the United States Government the winner all around.

Now I'll explain how we happened to get this Blickensderfer. One day I was at home, quietly minding my own business and trying to make both ends meet, when the doorbell rang. I answered it, and there stood a gentleman with a kindly face (and larceny in his heart).

"How do you do," he said. "Is Mr. Smith at home?"

"No, he isn't," I said, "but I'm Mrs. Smith. Can I help you?"

"No," he said. "I don't think so. I'm Mr. Minetta from the antique shop in White Plains, and I just happen to have something I think might interest Mr. Smith. Will you tell him I called?"

I didn't find it absolutely necessary to mention to Mr. Smith that Mr. Minetta had been by, but Mr. Minetta remembered to phone, and unfortunately my husband happened to answer the phone. Usually he just lies on the couch and lets me answer it, but on that particular day he happened to be feeling unusually active.

When the conversation ended after a few minutes, I could see on my husband's face a slight flush, a certain look of eager excitement that I recognized. He feigned disinterest.

"It's nothing," he said. "That was the man from that antique store in White Plains, you know, the one where I got the Moxie sign and those old planes and saws. He's got some rotten old typewriter he thought I'd want, but I don't want it. I told him I might come up and look at it tomorrow, but I won't go. It's silly. What do we need some busted up old typewriter for? Besides, we haven't got the money anyway for things like that."

Now as my husband is a writer and his office is right upstairs in our own house, he is not ordinarily in any particular hurry to get up in the morning and get to work. On that next morning, however, I was not too surprised to discover that he was up and dressed and down to breakfast before the children were ready.

"Up early this morning, aren't you?" I said as if I didn't suspect a thing.

"Well," he said, "there's nothing like getting up early and getting a good *start* on the day. I just feel as though I might get a lot of work done today."

He ate his breakfast quickly and almost broke a finger grabbing the car keys off the hook where we keep them.

"I think I'll just run over to the library," he said, keeping his voice as casual and offhand as he could. I happened to know that it was one of the late-opening days at the library, but as he never can remember which are the late days at our library, he didn't suspect that I suspected anything.

He returned, a half hour later, triumphantly carrying the Blickensderfer, also a metal box which said "Wills and Sons' FINE SHAGG Tobacco" which proved to contain metal dominoes, each of which has on its back, "Wills and Sons' FINE SHAGG Tobacco." Luckily he hadn't bought any more stereopticons as we already have two: one ordinary one that you hold in your hand and one giant carved mahogany one that was meant to have the place of honor on the parlor table, along with the Tiffany glass lamp, if you were rich folks.

I mean to say, Mr. Minetta is no fool. He isn't going to bother making special trips all the way from White Plains to people's houses without he's pretty sure he's going to make a sale. I think Mr. Minetta runs his store the way my husband runs his home. Any time anyone brings him any old junk, they're pretty sure they can sell it to him, because he's pretty sure he can sell it to Mr. Smith. When he goes off to auctions, he's not afraid to bid. Not Mr. Minetta. Why should he be? He can always sell it to Mr. Smith. He always *has*.

Now I have nothing against a good antique. We have

some pieces of antique furniture that I prize and a
few pieces of old china that I find very beautiful, and
I've even become attached to the Moxie sign in the
kitchen (gentleman bicyclist offers glass of Moxie to
lady bicyclist. "MOXIE?" he asks. "Certainly," she says,
"I just love it.") Yet when I look at the Blickensderfer
or the Oliver, nothing happens. All I can think of is,
how in the world are we ever going to get rid of that old
junk?

We did dispose of the Model A Ford after a while,
at a loss of only seventy-five dollars, because even my
husband could see that you couldn't fit a 1957 Ford and
a 1931 Ford, *and* two bicycles, lawn mowers, leaf sweep-
ers, rakes, shovels, summer furniture, and a washing-
machine crate that nobody would cart away, all in a
plain old two-car garage. We sold the Model A Ford to
a maniac from Cincinnati who insisted on driving it
home.

"Do you think I could drive it home?" he asked,
while he was examining the motor and trying to decide
whether to buy it or not.

"I wouldn't drive it to White Plains," my husband
answered.

"I wouldn't drive it to the corner," I put in, always
anxious to help make a sale.

He bought it, got stuck four times on the way home,
and then sent us a bitter little postcard remarking that
he'd had a lot of trouble, *as we very well knew he would.*
Not only had we lost seventy-five dollars on the deal,
but we had to take abuse too. Still, *we did get rid of
the thing,* with its damn original hubcaps and original

paint and half its original upholstery. But after all, how many maniacs can there be in Cincinnati?

What I really need is a nice little antique store in Mount Vernon, or New Rochelle, with a customer like Mr. Smith. Then I could sell *them* all *our* junk.

I almost made it the other day. A man came to our door insisting that he would buy *anything*.

"Old gold?" he said eagerly. "Old silver, old china? Jewelry? Watches? Typewriters?"

"Typewriters!" I said. "Come right *in*. I just happen to have some old typewriters." So I showed him the Oliver and the Blickensderfer.

"Lady," he said, shaking his head sadly, "what could I do with *those*?"

And that's what I want to know, too.

Confessions of a Rug Addict

I was born of well-to-do but honest parents. Of my early life I remember little except that I was comfortable and happy. There was no hint then of the tragic addiction that was to mar my adult life.

As a child I was normal in every respect, with no particular interest in rugs, except the specially prized Oriental rug of my mother's on which I spilled a whole bottle of red ink. This particular rug was more or less forced on my attention. My mother thought the rug looked nicer without the ink, but secretly I thought the ink a nice cheerful touch. In this opinion I was later corroborated when the rug, ink and all, brought a higher price at auction than any of the other, inkless, ones. (My mother believes it is possible that the price would have been even higher had the rug been without the inkstain, but she has always been conservative.)

It wasn't till a few years ago that it began. I was walking down the street one day, the very soul of innocence and with not even the slightest thought of rugs, when I happened to pass a needlework shop. There was a rug in the window and I stopped to look. Something came over me, and the next thing I knew, I was staggering home with a piece of canvas and ninety-seven skeins of rug wool.

The first rug I made was a small one, with a design of two birds with long tails, and it turned out so well and was so much admired that I thought I ought to make a second, larger one.

The second had a design of small squares, each square containing some small creature—snail, bird, spider, etc., with no repeats.

Having completed two rugs, fringe and all, with animals, I felt a strong urge to make a rug with fruit on it, and so the third one had a pear, an apple, some grapes and plums, and a few cherries. It was a smasher!

I bought more wool and more canvas, for I felt that now that I had the fruit one, I simply *had* to make a rug with two giraffes and a tree.

Unfortunately, it is difficult to buy rug makings that haven't a design already stamped on them, and I was always in such a hurry that I found myself working part of a giraffe, say, on top of a pattern of violent red and orange autumn leaves. It was hard. It involved a good deal of ripping out, and I used a lot of words highly unsuited to the ladylike occupation of making rugs.

When I made my first rug, I was very proud of it, and my husband liked it too. We had no trouble placing it— it just naturally went in front of the red leather wing chair. The second one was easy to place, too. It just belonged in front of the fireplace. The third one seemed to go nicely in front of the couch, with the coffee table standing on it, and the fourth went in front of the club chair.

By the fifth, we were doing considerable shifting from one foot to the other and muttering, "Why don't we try it in front of—no, it's too big. Why don't we try the—no, it would get in the way of the door."

Sometimes I am saddened when I think of the big green oval rug which we originally bought for the living room, because inch by inch and year by year it is being slowly lost in a quicksand of handmade rugs. I am saddened even more by the dreadful thought that soon my first prized rugs will themselves begin to be hidden by a new layer of later works. That is, I will soon have to scatter scatter rugs on the scatter rugs, and that gives me pause.

My husband is beginning to feel resentful. He has no one to talk to in the evening. He starts a conversation. "Say," he says, "there's a wonderful article in here about . . ." "Hand me that skein of green," I mutter.

I have often thought, since we have so many rugs, that it might be nice to give one away sometime, but when it comes right down to choosing which, I cannot do it. I love them all.

I could give it up by myself, but that pusher in the rug store makes trouble for me. After all, *he* knows I'm hooked.

I'm Not a Nice Lady

I never met the people from whom we bought our house. They were away for the summer when we saw it and decided to buy it; they came back briefly to remove their furniture and had moved out again several weeks before we moved in. They were an elderly couple who had built the house in 1909, raised a large family of children and grandchildren in it, and then decided to sell it when all their children had moved away and left them alone in the ten rooms.

That was all I knew about the Campbells when we moved into the house and started raising our own family.

We hardly had our hats and coats off when the first peddler rang the bell. His face fell when he saw me. "Where is Mrs. Campbell?" he asked. "The Campbells have moved to Connecticut," I explained. He shrugged and quickly opened a small black bag which I had not noticed before. It contained a grimy assortment of very shiny rayon ties with large machine stitching and frayed threads sticking out of the folds. "Only dollar-and-a-half, lady," he said. "Three dollar if you buy in store." I was not, at that time, acquainted with door-to-door salesmen. I had grown up in city apartments and this was a phase of suburban life with which I was poorly equipped to cope. I did not say "no" firmly, nor did I quite say "yes." As I hesitated, looking and feeling doubtful about the whole thing, the salesman shook his head sadly. "Mrs. Campbell," he said, "she was *nice* lady. She always buy my ties. Lots of ties." I finally bought one tie, as he had known right away I would, and made up my mind to be firmer in the future.

After the tie salesman came the kimono-tea-china-and-slippers man. "Mrs. Campbell *always* buy from me," he said. "Much tea, many slipper, kimono." I bought, for a dollar and a half, a quarter of a pound of singularly bitter tea.

88

Next came the linen tablecloth lady. "Oh, I'm so *sorry* Mrs. Campbell moved away," she said pettishly. "She was my best customer." As the tablecloths were really expensive and as I never use tablecloths at all, I really did say no, and meant it. "Mrs. Campbell *knew quality*," said the linen tablecloth lady, looking at me with disdain. "The Campbells used lots of tablecloths and they always bought new ones from me." It was clear that anyone who stooped to place mats (and sometimes even plastic or paper mats, at that) was hardly fit to live in the same house that had sheltered the Campbells.

Next came the lady who sold pot holders and aprons. By then my "no" was getting firmer and quicker. She looked sad. "Where is Mrs. Campbell?" she asked despondently. "She always bought my aprons and pot holders. Lots of pot holders and aprons she buy. *She* was a *nice* lady."

Over the years they came in hordes, in droves, in coveys, in packs, selling hairpins, magazines, brushes, vacuum cleaners, roofing, rugs, beautiful imported English tweeds, pincushions, encyclopedias, and all agreed, "Mrs. Campbell, *she* was *nice* lady."

Shortly after we moved in, all the plaster started cracking, and we called in the man who had done the plastering and painting. "Well," he said accusingly, "I've been doing work in this house for forty years and nothing like *that* ever happened before. The Campbells hardly ever turned on the heat," he said, "and you come in here and turn on the heat like this, and of *course* your plaster is going to crack."

The living-room floor started to sag where the piano was. "Well," said the flooring man, "naturally. The

Campbells had a spinet piano. You come in here with a big old upright and naturally your floor is going to sag."

Fuses blew. "Well of course," said the wiring man. "The Campbells had hardly any electrical equipment. You bring in a washing machine and a dishwasher and all those lamps and it stands to reason the fuses are going to blow."

I don't suppose I shall ever meet Mrs. Campbell, but I would certainly like to. I try to picture her in her home in Connecticut. She is now quite old I imagine, and I see her sitting quietly in a rocker, browsing a bit in one of her encyclopedias. She is wearing a Japanese kimono and slippers, an apron, and she has on her hand a pot-holder mitt. She is sipping bitter tea, and the table at her side is covered with a large gleaming white linen cloth. A billowing white linen napkin is draped on her knees. The cup and saucer are Japanese, with lots of gold and flowers. She reads by the light of a candle to avoid blowing fuses, and under the kimono she wears several sweaters as the house is entirely unheated except for one small stove. A guitar rests very lightly on the floor. Mr. Campbell is there, too, reading from a Children's Book Shelf and wearing a shiny frayed rayon tie. They both have very kind faces, well creased and weather-worn. They are resting, now, because they are very tired from answering the doorbell.

I Don't Know My Name
but the Face Is Familiar

I was not considered unusually stupid in school, but there are certain things that I cannot seem to learn. I am now twenty-eight years old, and have been twenty-eight for some eleven years, so you would think that I could have learned most of the ordinary everyday type of information needed for living. I was able, with little difficulty, to learn to find the volume of a truncated pyramid, to spell "truncated pyramid," to memorize the principal products of Portugal and several irregular French verbs. However, I cannot learn which months have thirty days and which have thirty-one. I get along all right with February, but when it comes to August or March or December, I'm lost. Eleven times a year I have to recite "Thirty days hath September" to myself to find out if it's time to set my calendar clock forward or pay the mortgage.

I have a phenomenal memory for telephone numbers. I can, without recourse to a directory, phone anyone I have ever called before, no matter how many years have elapsed. Yet, if I should need a new number, I cannot call Information. I try. I wrinkle my brow, chew my tongue, wring my hands, squint my eyes, and utter little moans. But it's no use. I cannot remember Information's number.

I'm a whiz at grasping the principles of latitude and longitude and equinoxes and date lines and ecliptics and orbits and time zones. But when it comes to daylight saving time, I cannot remember whether to set the clocks forward or back, and, whichever it turns out to be, whether the result will then be to give us an extra hour or leave us an hour short. Year after year I keep my children up an hour later on the night we set the clocks ahead, only to discover the following morning that I was wrong again and they're hollow-eyed and sleepy. Some years I set the clocks the wrong way and get angry at the friends who were supposed to come for lunch at one o'clock and don't arrive till three and then don't even *apologize*. It's careless of them. They should have left the house earlier, or at least phoned. How should *I* know the clocks should have been set forward?

I have a gift for languages and I'm a brilliant amateur philologist. I can tell you the derivation of satrap, sapphire, or sarsaparilla without a moment's hesitation. I know the Greek alphabet. I can spell "scacchic." But if I want to look up "scacchic" in the dictionary, I have to recite, inside my head, "a, b, c, d, e, f, g..." all the way to "s," or else I don't know where to look in the dictionary.

As a matter of fact, I can't remember my own age, although I was awfully good at algebra. I have to think of the year I was born, and subtract it from the calendar year. It often takes several minutes and it's embarrassing.

Especially in view of the fact that I have a marvelous memory for dates.

I've been driving a car for twenty years and I've never had an accident or a ticket. I haven't even run over anybody yet. I know all about how a car engine works and where the distributor is and what the crankshaft is. But I cannot remember what that little knob is right there. Is it the heater? Or the radio? Is it possibly for the headlights? Or is it the cigarette lighter? Maybe it's the ventilator. Is is perhaps the switch that turns on the light in the glove compartment? *I* don't know.

Is my dentist appointment next Tuesday? Or is it Friday?

Do you say "dived" or "dove?"

What's my name?

And all right, "scacchic" means pertaining to chess.

Dinner en Famille

(GENTLE TINKLE OF SILVER DINNER BELL)
(LONG SILENCE)
Must they all disappear every night exactly at dinner-time?
(LOUD PERSISTENT RINGING OF BELL)
Oh, there you are, dear. Would you call the children? Dinner is ready. Thanks.
Have you washed your hands, boys? Well please do. I don't care if you washed them this morning, that

doesn't make them clean now. Go on, children, hurry up. Will you carve for me, honey, while the children wash? I'll get everything else on the table. What's the matter with that knife? I know it isn't sharp. I asked you to sharpen it for me last week, darling. When you get a chance will you please sharpen it for me? Well here, try this knife. I know it's a paring knife. I know it's too small. The other carving knife has disappeared, darling. You borrowed it one day to do something to the lawn mower and you never brought it back.

Please! The children will hear you.

Oh, there you are, boys. Well, let me see your hands. Joe! Did you wash your hands at all? Well, you didn't wash the backs. What *is* all that blue sticky stuff? Well, go wash them again. Dan, let me see yours. Well, I don't care if you washed them in lye, they're still dirty.

What's the matter with the meat, honey? The meat isn't tough. It's that knife. Well, you'll just have to do the best you can. Honey.

Don't touch that platter, it's hot. Oh. Hurt much, dear? Dan, run upstairs for me and bring down the burn ointment, that's an angel. I know there should be a tube of burn ointment in the kitchen, darling. I always keep one here. Right in this drawer. But it isn't here now. Didn't you take it down to the cellar one day when you burned yourself while you were soldering something? Well, you never brought it back, darling.

All right, boys, sit down. Darling, sit down and I'll serve. Everything will get cold if we don't start. Dan, your napkin is on the floor, darling, pick it up. Joe, don't put your milk glass so close to the edge of the table, sweetheart.

94

I know you don't like carrots, darling, but you don't like peas, string beans, spinach, beets, turnips, or cauliflower either. So it's hard to know what to have. Here, have some celery.

Now let me see. You want it rare, dear, don't you. I know you like it well done, Joe. *Very* well done. I know, honey. And very rare for you, Dan. It is too rare. If it were any rarer it would be raw. Darling, you want gravy on your meat but not on your potatoes? Dan, you want gravy just on your potatoes? Joe, you want gravy just on your *carrots*? Joe dear, move the glass back from the edge of the table. Well, there now, I think we're all set. Oh, I forgot the rolls. Here they are. Have a roll, darling? I know they're burned. It took you all so long to come to dinner, honey. They're only burned a little. Well, eat the inside. I'll just get my coffee. Darling, do you want your coffee now or later? You want *grape juice?* Joe, you want grape juice too? Dan, I suppose you . . . oh, you want apple juice. Well, you all go ahead and I'll. . . . There we are. Grape juice for you, Dan, pick your napkin up off the floor, darling, grape juice for you, apple juice for you. Joe, push your glass back, honey. Joe, cut your meat with your *knife* and *fork*. You're ready for seconds, Dan? I haven't had a first yet. You take your plate and help yourself from the platter. Watch out for Joe's gla—oh. Don't just sit there and let the milk drip in your lap, Joe. *Stand up.* On your shoes, Dan? Well, why didn't you stand back? Here, I'll get a cloth. Just lift the cream pitcher up for me, Joe. Right there, darling. *Right there.* Oh, *Joe.* I know you didn't *mean* to drop it. Milk on your new pants, darling? Here, I'll get this all cleaned up. Dan, just get the container of cream from the icebox and fill the pitcher again for me. Right there, dear, on the top shelf. See, right in back of the tomato ju—oh no. DANNY, STEP BACK. DON'T JUST STAND THERE IN IT. Here, I'll take care of it. Now everybody sit down and eat your dinner. Joe, don't hit the ketchup bottle so hard, let Daddy do it for y— Yes, I see it got in the sugar, sweetheart. Darling, will you help Dan to some more meat while I just finish cleaning up this tomato juice? Joe, it *isn't necessary* to butter both sides of the bread. What is it, dear? The meat slipped off the platter? I know, darling. It's on account of that knife. Well, pick it up off the stove and put it back on the platter. Now let's all sit down and *enjoy our dinner*. Joe, you eat string beans with a fork. I know Mommy lets you pick up asparagus with your fingers and dangle it into your mouth, but not string beans. String beans are different, that's why. Why can't you eat the meat, Joe? It has a speck of fat on it? Where? Well, for heaven's sake cut it off. No, it *hasn't* spoiled the potatoes. What's wrong with your salad, Dan? That's chicory. That's tomato. That's escarole. That's cucumber. That's radish. That's romaine lettuce. That little speck? That's a tiny bit of chopped hard-boiled egg that I always fix for Daddy's salad. A tiny bit got into the salad bowl by mistake. You can't eat the salad? Well just don't eat that little speck of egg. Put it on the side of your plate. It *has not* spoiled the lettuce.

What is it, darling? There's ketchup on the butter? I hadn't noticed. There's ketchup in the sugar too. There's a little in my coffee, too, but *I'm* not complaining. There's some on your meat, Joe? Well, you put it there. Well, why did you use it if you don't like ketchup? Danny, please pick up your napkin. It's on the floor. Joe, you're kicking Mommy's leg, darling. Well, don't. *Don't*. Don't *kick* Mommy's leg, angel. No, darling, that's not the table leg. That's *my* leg. Yes, sweetheart, that's what I was trying to tell you. Dan, would you *please* pick up your napkin and also pass the gravy? *Not at the same time.* Sweetheart, couldn't you see that if you bent over to pick up the napkin, the gravy was going to spill? No, darling, the gravy boat isn't attached to the plate it's on. I know it should be, angel, but Joe broke it last week when he was making plaster molds in it. Darling, you're not eating your salad. You don't feel like salad tonight? But you'd just like some sliced tomatoes. What's the matter, Joe? You don't like mixed salad? You'd rather have plain lettuce and Russian dressing? Well, Mommy can't fix all different things for everybody, can she? Well, I know I'm slicing tomatoes for Daddy. *Well, that's different, that's why.*

Well. There now. Everybody ready for dessert? I've made a really special dessert tonight. Something good. You'll like it, Joe. Yes you *will*. It's chocolate, darling. You like chocolate, don't you? It's a sort of chocolate mousse. What don't you like about the way it looks? Well, you can't tell how it's going to taste by looking at it. No you *can't*. Dan, please get up and *carefully* help clear the table. I know there isn't room there, sweetheart. Put them on the counter by the sink. No no, not on top of the . . . Dan, couldn't you see that all those plates were going to fall if you put them on top of a tomato? I know the tomato shouldn't have been there, darling, but it was left over when I was slicing them for Daddy. I know Daddy should have eaten the mixed salad. Because that's different, that's why. Joe, push your milk glass back from the edge of the table. Dan, please don't put the glasses down in the mashed potatoes. *Because I say not to.* Dan, you forgot to take the butter dish. Joe, you take the salad plates. Well, darling, if there's tomato juice on the floor there don't walk in it. Go around the other way. You can't go around the other way? There's milk on that side. Maybe we all ought to wear galoshes to dinner. Now everybody sit down and I'll serve the dessert. What is it, darling? You're not hungry tonight? You'd rather have canned peaches? What is it, Joe? What don't you like about it? You like ice cream better? Well we're not having ice cream tonight. Homemade mousse is better than ice cream. *I* say it is. What is it, Dan? It tastes of egg? Of course it does. It has egg in it. You don't like eggs? You *love* eggs. Oh. You only like them scrambled. I know Daddy's having peaches. Because that's different, that's why. Oh all right. You can both have ice cream. Let's see, there's butter pecan, vanilla, strawberry, pineapple, chocolate-chip mocha. Well, there isn't any plain chocolate. No, there isn't any vanilla fudge, either. All right, Dan, you want half chocolate-chip mocha and half pineapple? Joe, you want half vanilla and half butter pecan? Can't you get together on it? Oh for heaven's sake. All right. Dan, pick up your napkin. There isn't any chocolate-chip mocha, Dan. Somebody put an empty carton back in the freezer. Who did? A baby sitter. Oh. Joe, this isn't vanilla, it's coffee. Well somebody put the vanilla top on the coffee carton. Well I can't help that, I didn't do it. The baby sitter. I know you're not babies, it's just an expression.

Dan, please pick up your napkin, darling. Joe, push your glass back, angel. Here are your peaches, darling. You'd kind of like a fruit compote? Where is there gravy on my dress? You wish we had some cake, Dan? I see the ketchup, but I don't see any gravy. (LONG PIERCING SCREAM)

Some Wistful Thoughts of a Woman About to Sit Down

I suppose there are some people who sit down with a calm feeling of confidence that they are about to land on the soft, well-upholstered cushion of a chair.

In my house you sit down with a little thrill of nervous excitement and panic. As you pass the point of no return, at which gravity inexorably pulls you down, you think, "Did I see a flash of something metal on that chair?" but it's too late. You did. And at the next moment you land, painfully, on somebody's little electric hand generator. This is not good for you, the generator, or the chair cushion.

Of course it isn't always a generator. It might be a battery with wires sticking out of it. Or a piece of telescope somebody just put down for a minute. Or a not-quite-finished model ship (with the masts already set in place). Or a butterfly net (with a butterfly in it). Or a compass. Even a protractor. Or a coping saw. Large shears. A wrench. A Viking helmet with its two horns pointing up.

Sometimes it isn't even anything hard. Then it's even worse. It could just be a stuffed animal, but on the other hand it *could* be a cat (alive), or a hamster that has unaccountably escaped from his cage, or a handful of water beetles that somebody brought from the pond and is loving up, only he just left them there for a minute while he went to get a Coke.

As a matter of fact, there isn't anything it *couldn't* be.

I am a person who believes that one should try to experience everything that life has to offer. I therefore hope that some day before I die, I may have the luxury, just once, of sitting down on a chair, and I won't even *ask* for a mink coat.

More Domestic Definitions

More Domestic Definitions

The Floor

The floor is a smooth piece of wood that keeps the walls apart. It also keeps you from falling right through into the basement where you could very possibly hurt yourself.

The floor is very handy for retrieving fallen objects. It stops them at the exact level of your feet where you can easily pick them up or kick them into a corner.

The floor makes a marvelous space on which to put furniture. If it were not for the floor, it would be very hard to keep the furniture nice and level, and if you don't keep your furniture nice and level it's very uncomfortable when you want to sit down.

A floor helps to make the rugs and carpets lie flat. Everyone knows there is nothing more unsightly than a wrinkled rug. A floor adds years to the life of your rugs. I hardly even know where you'd *put* them without a floor.

The floor is the very best place there is to play jacks. And it is also a fine place to put your trash baskets.

Not only does the floor work for you, it also makes a dandy place for the people on the floor below to hang their chandeliers from. Or even mobiles, if they're the kind of people who like mobiles.

And perhaps most important of all, if you had no

floor, you would always be flicking your cigarette ashes on the heads of the people below and wouldn't that be messy? Especially as the people above would be flicking *theirs* on *you*.

The Roof

The roof is the thing on top of the house to which you attach a television aerial. It is also a good place to put a chimney. How would it look if the chimney came out sideways through the wall? It would spoil the entire line of the house and make the architect *sick*.

A roof assures privacy from people in taller houses or airplanes, or telephone linemen and flagpole sitters. It would be horrid to have no roof and have all those people staring in.

A roof is an effective screen against leaves, twigs, acorns, apples, walnuts, squirrels, bird feathers, possibly even birds, and heaven only knows what all kinds of trash. A house without a roof would get very untidy.

A roof prevents the living-room couch from getting sopping wet every time it rains or snows, and in the winter the house might get very cold without one.

The roof is a good place from which to hang gutters, and if you like dormer windows you absolutely could not have one without a roof.

A roof is a good thing to have. You could almost consider it a necessity.

The Bed

A bed is an oblong soft flat thing which eliminates the necessity of sleeping in a chair where you would be very cramped. Or of sleeping on the floor and getting up in the morning all over bruises and in a foul humor.

A bed is composed of three parts: a frame, made of wood or metal, a box spring which is set into the frame, and a mattress which is too heavy to turn over. The whole thing is set on legs which keep it just high enough off the floor so you can lose things under it, but not high enough to clean under it. (What's that under there? A *butter* knife?)

One of the most important functions of the bed is, of course, for smoothing out the bedspread. Where else can you smooth out a bedspread? And who wants a wrinkled spread? Goodness!

The bed provides a place to sit on the side of while you're talking on the phone. It is also a good place to lie with your head hanging down to see what things look like upside down. And there is no better place for the kiddies to do their homework, paint pictures, model clay, run railroads, spill ink, and crumble crayons. You wouldn't want them to do it on the floor, would you? It would make an awful mess to sweep up.

A bed is an excellent trampoline, and there is no better way to develop co-ordination than practice on the trampoline. Besides, you certainly wouldn't want to use the couch—it could break the springs.

If you had no bed, you would have a big empty space right there in the bedroom. It wouldn't look nice at all. It would look as though you'd forgotten something when you were furnishing the room. And where would you put your sheets and blankets? And where in heaven's name would you put your feet when you wanted to lie down?

The bed is the place where you lay your clothes when you clean out your closet. It is also where you put the suitcases when you're packing. It is the place to lay out the laundry to sort it. It is the place to dump packages when you come home from shopping. It is where you put the top of the sewing machine when you're sewing.

The bed is what you throw your bathrobe on the foot of when you go to sleep.

Without a bed, the bottom sheet would probably get very rumpled and you would toss and turn all night. You probably wouldn't get any sleep at all.

Just before you go to sleep, and you're reading and smoking a last cigarette, the bed catches all the cigarette sparks. Otherwise they might fall on the floor and set the whole house on fire. A bed *is* a comfort.

Porch steps are nice.

Porch Steps

Porch steps are made of rotten wood and peeling paint and consist of a series of planes alternately perpendicular or parallel to the ground. They connect the house to the ground and greatly facilitate entry to the house. Without them you might have to get a little stepladder or build a little ramp. At the very least, you would have to be very athletic.

Porch steps are where you sit down to pant and light a cigarette when you've been raking leaves or shoveling snow. Porch steps are where you sit to put on roller skates. Porch steps are where you leave the stilts lying up on. Porch steps are where you lean the bicycle on.

Porch steps provide a series of flat surfaces on which all kinds of things can be placed: a pile of books, a half-eaten jelly apple, the leaf rake, rocks that look as though they might be pretty when scrubbed clean, just plain rocks, shoes, cameras, sweaters, jars of caterpillars, cats, kittens, etc. You can put almost anything on the porch steps. You can leave a can of paint and a tire pump there. But I'll be furious if you do. What do you think this is, the town dump?

In the winter when the sun melts the ice and snow on the roof and it drips from the eaves and gutters only to refreeze on the ground, the porch steps catch it. With-

107

out the porch steps there to catch it, the ice might form on the walk, and someone could slip and fall.

Porch steps are nice.

The Automobile

An automobile is a machine with four wheels, a motor, and not quite enough seats, which enables people to get about with great rapidity and ease to places they never bothered going to before and where they'd just as soon not be now, because now that they're there, there's no place to park.

This machine is so ingeniously contrived that you don't have to know anything at all to manipulate the controls. In driving the modern car, the only part of you that is likely to get tired is your forefinger. (This is hard on housewives who need full use of that finger to run the dishwasher.)

Sometimes the automobile carries you in minutes distances that would have taken days with a horse. However, should it be a holiday or a weekend, it sometimes carries you in hours distances that would have taken minutes with a horse. I've spent more time at the Bronx Whitestone Bridge than a horse's normal life span. Sometimes I think it's more than my normal life span.

Having an automobile is almost like having wings. Except for one thing: it isn't the least bit like having wings. The only thing that's like having wings is being the man in the helicopter who's flying around taking pictures of the traffic backed up for thirteen miles at the Lincoln Tunnel.

Most cars cost a great deal of money, while others cost a *great* deal of money. You can easily spend ten thousand dollars on a car.* This is too bad when you consider that there is no such thing as having a new car. As soon as you *have* it, it is a secondhand car.

Automobiles come in shades of pink, lavender, chartreuse, cerulean blue, apricot, and azalea trimmed lavishly from front to tail with chrome. If you're hit by a car, it makes it all so much gayer. Black is a depressing color.

* I can too, but not easily.

Arithmetic Problem

I can never understand," complains my husband bitterly, "why it is that women never have enough frankfurter rolls for the number of frankfurters." He thinks I buy the wrong number of rolls in the market because I can't add.

What he doesn't understand, and I wish this information could be disseminated to all disgruntled husbands who have just been reluctantly told that although there are two more frankfurters, there are no more rolls, is that no matter how carefully you market, there can't *be* as many rolls as frankfurters. This is one of the sad facts of life. In this great, madly efficient country of ours, where the frank in a roll is a national mania, the frankfurter people and the roll people have never gotten together to co-ordinate the number of franks in a package with the number of rolls in a package. It may be that there is some kind of a feud going on between the meat packers and the bakers. *I* don't know. All I know is, I buy a package of franks and there are eight, nine, or ten in the package. And packages of rolls have either six or eight. Then after we've eaten them all up, my husband sees the two leftover franks lying there and he says, "I think maybe I could eat one more," and then when I tell him there are no more rolls, he says,

"For heaven's sake, why can't women ever have enough rolls for the frankfurters?" I tried buying two packages of rolls, but then he said, "How is it there are never enough frankfurters for the rolls?" You can't win.

What I wish is that the frankfurter industry and the bakery industry would patch up their quarrel and get together. Six franks in a package and six rolls. Or eight franks in a package and eight rolls. Or *something*. This is *awful*.

I Don't Ask Much

I was walking down the street the other day on my way to the bakery, minding my own business, not bothering anybody, not littering the sidewalk, not making unnecessary noise, being a perfectly decent law-abiding honest citizen, when a lady stopped me.

"Your stockings are falling down," she said.

I stared.

"Your stockings are falling down," she said again. "I thought maybe you didn't know."

Now what did she have to go and do that for? *I* knew my stockings were falling down. I mean I'm not unconscious or anything. I just happened to choose not to notice that my stockings were falling down. Once I admitted that I knew they were falling down, I'd have to stop and pull them up, and that doesn't look nice.

As long as nobody actually stopped and pointed it out to me, I could just go my happy way to the bakery pretending I didn't know.

Besides, what was she fussing about? She was lucky I wasn't losing a shoe or a hem. Can I help it if I'm not neat?

Somebody is always taking the joy out of life. One day as I was going out, I noticed three men standing in the middle of the street staring at my house.

"Something wrong?" I said.

One of them laughed. "That your house?" he asked on what I thought was a rather contemptuous note.

"It is," I said, bridling.

"Well," he said, "we were just lookin' how it's saggin' there in the middle. Boy," he went on, "you don't get that porch shored up, you're in trouble. Just *look* at that."

I know the porch needs shoring up. Shoring up nothing, it needs rebuilding. It just so happens we need a new oil burner, too. And the roof needs fixing. And the whole house needs a coat of paint. And the children's bureaus are falling apart. And the blankets are seventeen years old. And the living-room rug has a hole in it. Does he *have* to stand there and point it out to me? Maybe I should have invited him in, so he could go on a tour of the house and show me all the places where the wallpaper is coming loose.

The other day I was parking my car in the village (I know, I know—there's a dent in the front fender) when a man pulled up beside me and shouted, "Hey lady, you can't park there, that's a loading zone."

I knew it was a loading zone. Did he think I was

driving around blindfolded? I saw the sign. But it just so happened I didn't feel like seeing that sign at that particular moment. Did he ever think of *that* before he decided to make himself such a good Samaritan? I'll bet if I'd been stuck on the parkway with a flat tire he suddenly wouldn't have been such a do-gooder. It's none of his business if I just don't happen to notice a sign. Let him watch out for his own driving. He nearly backed into that old lady, he was so anxious to point that sign out to me.

The other night my husband came home and for some unexplained reason happened to look at our children's feet.

"Gee," he said, "look at their *shoes*. They're a *disgrace*."

Well, *I* knew *that*. They've been that way for months. So the heels *are* run over a little. So they *need* shines. All right, so they need new shoes. But they were happy. Their little faces were absolutely shining with happiness. And they're fairly clean. And they're well fed. And they're healthy. And they've had every shot there is. And they get a vitamin pill every morning. And they have warm coats for the winter. And mittens. And ice skates. And cameras. And watches. And good allowances. And radios. So their shoes *are* a little worn out. There were no holes in their *socks*. So why did he have to point it out to me? I knew their shoes were a sight. Now I have to take them all the way to White Plains, and I won't find a parking space, and they'll complain every inch of the way because they had some damn project they wanted to work on, and they don't even like to buy new shoes, and I'll have to drive around for a half-hour looking for a place to park, and the store will be hot and crowded, and everybody will be perfectly miserable. And it will cost twenty dollars. And the salesman will sell me new rubbers and galoshes and sneakers and bedroom slippers and socks, and instead of twenty dollars it will be forty dollars. And everybody was *perfectly happy*. So *why* did he have to mention it?

I know I need a haircut. *I* know the car needs a wash. *I* know that apple tree needs pruning. *I* know my handbag is open and a handkerchief is falling out. *I* know I just missed the train, lady. I see it, I see it.

So would you all mind awfully just leaving me be?

Bloody but Bowed

I've just made a new rule in my house. Hereafter, anyone who bleeds is on his own. I'm sick and tired of making tourniquets and bandages and mopping floors, and I will not go into that emergency room at our local hospital any more.

I have a small but intense family of people who never do anything dangerous. They don't play baseball or football or even move around a lot. Mostly they sit and read quietly, draw pictures, make model ships, and play records. Our house, I feel sure, would easily pass all the safety tests thought up by the Safety Council. Our stairs are clean, solid, and well lighted, cellar and attic well ventilated and free from rubbish, wiring kept up to date, and tools neatly stored on a pegboard. Yet somehow doorways suddenly hit people on the head, saws leap from their moorings and cut thumbs, bicycles shy at a bit of paper and throw their riders, beds tilt and dump their occupants on the floor, cellar doors trip people up, and off I go, with a child or husband in tow, leaving a trail of blood all the way to the hospital.

We used to have a tan car in which I took my bleeding relatives to the hospital, but passers-by on the street shrieked so, we gave it up and got a bright red car. That helped a little. Now I'm thinking of carpeting the whole house in red and redoing all the furniture with nice red covers.

The rallying cry that goes echoing through my house is, "How many stitches?" I think there's a contest to see who can get the most sewing done, but I'm not sure who's supposed to give the prize. When they're not counting stitches (you'd think they were making sweaters), it's, "How long must the plaster cast stay on?"

I know every surgeon and orthopedist in Westchester County, and I have a nodding acquaintance with batches of them in New York. As soon as they see us, without a word they start soaking their plaster and threading their needles. *They* know.

The quieter the house is, the more I wait for the cry of "Oooooo, eeeeee," that accompanies the new flow of blood and the new wound which I must inspect and decide whether to attempt to stick up with bandage and adhesive tape or get properly sewed up. I don't even know why we bother to keep bandages around the house. We haven't used them in years. The emergency room at the hospital is well equipped for the necessary dressings, and we usually arrive there with my best guest towels stanching the flow.

I have become so accustomed to these little crises that the last time we had a broken bone at three o'clock in the morning (somebody fell out of bed) I inspected it, remarked lightly, "Oh well, you've just broken your collarbone again," and went back to sleep.

Yet through all this welter of bandages and plaster, I am the one member of the family who, in spite of daily handling of sharp knives, hot fat, flame, and scissors, never has a wound. So I'm resigning as medical head of this household, and from now on they can go on the street to bleed and hail a kindhearted passing motorist to get them to the hospital.

I'm All Thumbs
(but None of Them Is Green)

When I lived in the city I had a chronic and frustrating struggle with a sick philodendron, a stunted ivy, and a couple of melancholy begonias. There was nothing fundamentally wrong with my care, I felt. The trouble arose from an apartment so situated that only moss or a nice crop of mushrooms could have flourished. In fact, not only was the apartment unfit for plant life, it was not very fit for humans, either.

When we moved to the country it was early winter, and since I couldn't do any planting outdoors, even before the towels were put away and the dishes unpacked, I rushed out to a greenhouse and carried home everything but the glass roof. Every table, window sill, and shelf was covered with pots of plants—plants that trailed and plants that grew up, plants with smooth leaves and plants with hairy leaves, big plants and little plants. My brand new custom-built kitchen with the Formica counter tops was so crowded with greenery that I could hardly find a place to mix a cake, and we often found things in the salad that were not lettuce or chicory.

I was ecstatic. I was even more ecstatic as the months went by, for there wasn't a sick plant in the house. Every one had firm stems and glossy leaves, and they all grew happily, put out new shoots, and preened themselves all day long.

Everything was fine until one day when my husband noticed a book in the public library about the care of house plants. With the kindest of intentions he brought it home for me. That was when the trouble started.

I soon learned that none of the pots was the right kind or size for its occupant. Plants that should have been in south windows were in north windows, and vice versa. Our heating system was the wrong kind. And my method of watering the plants—which was simply to go around putting water in any pot that looked dry—was unscientific. Furthermore my plants were growing in just any old kind of dirt, whereas each plant should have been in soil prepared to a strict recipe just for *it*.

They were entirely unprepared for attack by plant lice, and they were unfertilized and uncultivated.

In short, there seemed to be more to growing house plants than I had dreamed, and I promptly set about correcting my mistakes.

I went about, daily, rapping pots with my knuckles to hear by the sound if the earth was dry, and then hefting them carefully to judge by the weight if the earth was dry, and even, once in a while, turning them out to examine the root ball. This was all a little bit like my opening the hood of the car to examine the motor when anything seems funny. I do it all the time to impress standers-by. I liked to examine my root balls when there were people around, and I would murmur "hm" and "aha," put them back, and throw some water in the pot. I moved all the plants around to give them the right amounts of sun and shade, and I didn't dare turn on the heat for fear of killing them with excessive dryness. I sprayed the leaves against aphids, and I got some well-rotted two-year-old manure, peat moss, fine sand, bone meal, lime, potash and made up recipes. Our own meals meanwhile, became slightly haphazard and leaned heavily on things in cans. Those plants needed more care than the children.

I thought I was really getting somewhere when suddenly we were afflicted with damping-off. Next the soil got moldy, the plants became pot-bound, the leaves turned yellow, we were infested with aphids, and in practically no time at all we were surrounded by large quantities of terribly dead flora.

The next time I see a book that tells how to do anything, I think I'll restrain myself and get a nice mystery instead. And in the meantime, does anyone want a flowerpot?

Watch Out for the Camellias!

ow that spring is in the air and the seed catalogues are in the mail, it's the time for every writer with enough strength to push down a typewriter key to write the annual piece about gardening. They write of their renewed hopes each spring as they study the catalogues, their subsequent struggles with weather, pests, blights, insects, and fertilizer, and their eventual and inevitable frustration when summer comes and they end up with the same messy old weed patch.

Not me. I'm *glad* when nothing comes up. Glad, do you hear me, glad, glad, glad!

I too used to have my little dreams and my big weeds, and I was sorry, because I grew up in the city in the Depression. The only time you could hope to have a lot of flowers was at your funeral. If a boy brought you flowers when he called for you, it was like getting a diamond ring. Flowers! You were lucky if you didn't have to feed him, pay for his subway fare, and lend him five bucks till next payday. Once a boy brought me one camellia. I never got over it.

I used to *like* flowers.

But last year we were in California. We had moved there at the end of the previous summer, and my husband had rented a house which had, among other things (other things being a rental that kept us awake nights, a gas furnace that never quite heated the house, and a sort of Olde Englishe architectural arrangement that effectively excluded all light and air), a Garden. The Garden made me pretty nervous when I first saw it, because I didn't know how the landlord would feel about having his Garden transformed into the biggest jungle in the San Fernando Valley, but when I learned that a Japanese gardener who came once a week was included in the rent, I felt better. I was also struck dumb. Me, the slum dweller, with a gardener!

We had, in our Garden, roses as big as chrysanthemums, begonias as big as sunflowers, lemon trees, orange trees, tangerine and grapefruit trees. And we had five bushes of camellias. We were too late for the flowering of the camellias, and I could hardly wait out the winter so I could see for myself just one camellia come to bud and then flower.

Of course it didn't *really* freeze that winter, but ice did form all over everything every night. Very likely the laws of physics are different in California and water freezes at a much higher temperature than back home. But I did worry about the camellias.

Then spring came, and all five camellia bushes put out buds. I was so excited that for one day I almost forgot to hate California. Every morning I rushed out to the patio to look at the camellia buds. There seemed to be quite a lot of them, so I felt pretty sure we'd get at least one flower.

When the day came, we looked at the flower for a long time. It was beautiful. It was pale pink and quite large and quite perfect. I took a picture of it.

The next day there were quite a few camellias. A neighbor told me that you have to pick them as they appear, so I picked them and had enough for a quite nice little centerpiece for the dining-room table. I sat right down to write letters home about it.

The next day there were enough camellias to fill a large bowl for the living room. I spent a good deal of time arranging them.

The day after that there were really a lot of camellias. I had to spend quite a bit of time hunting up bowls, and I put a bowl of camellias in each bedroom. I spent a little less time on the arrangements and I didn't stop to take any pictures.

The next day there were masses of camellias, and as they seemed to last quite a long time in the house, and the very first bowlful in the dining room still looked quite fresh, I spent most of the morning delivering camellias to all the neighbors. Lunch was a little late.

The day after that there were masses and masses of camellias, and I hardly knew where to start. It took quite a while just to cut them, let alone put them in bowls or arrange them. I finally gathered together all the kitchen bowls and filled them, and just put them around on any tables I could find. We had lunch at two o'clock, but I didn't have time to do the baby's laundry.

The following day the bushes were really quite covered with blossoms, and a lot had fallen on the ground. I didn't have time to pick them up. I started throwing out the first batches in the house, although they were still perfectly fresh. The garbage pail got quite full, and I had to carry a lot out to the incinerator and burn them. I noticed that the house was getting pretty dusty, but I didn't have time to dust.

It was on the next day that my enthusiasm for camellias began to wane. It took considerable time to sweep up the blossoms that had fallen on the ground, where they were beginning to look a little messy, and as the house was already quite full of camellias, I simply took them directly to the incinerator. Dinner that night was hardtack and pemmican.

When the gardener came the next morning, he set to work without a word, sweeping up the flowers and carrying load after load to the incinerator, but when he left, they were piling up again pretty fast, and my little boy began to complain that they were getting tangled in his tricycle wheels, and I was having trouble with the baby's carriage. I couldn't find time to make the beds that day.

The next day I began to worry. I was afraid they might get beyond us. I was glad we had a second story so that if the piles of camellias got past the first-floor windows, we would still be able to get air. I noticed, too, that the children's hair needed shampooing, but I couldn't take time from my sweeping and burning to do anything about it. I thought of calling on the Sanitation Department for emergency assistance, but when I thought about how much trouble we had just getting them to carry away a little garbage once in a while, I gave up that idea. Besides I didn't have time to stop for phone calls.

Every morning as I opened my eyes, I clutched my

husband's pajama sleeve (which he didn't like because he doesn't wear pajamas) and said, "I can't look. Are they past the windows yet?"

A simple solution finally presented itself. There *was* a way out.

We boarded a plane and came back East.

Oh, I study the seed catalogues, all right. And then I laugh and laugh as I throw them in the trash basket. I guess *I* know when I'm well off.

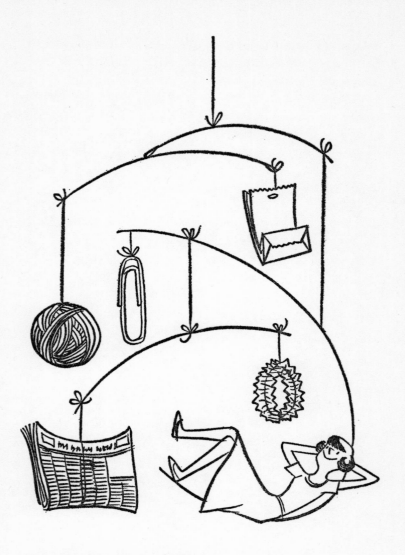

Last Domestic Definitions

Paper Clips

A paper clip is a little piece of wire that has unaccountably got all twisted up. It can be used to hold two pieces of paper together. It can also be untwisted and twisted again into other shapes if you find time on your hands.

A paper clip is exactly the right size and weight for throwing into ceiling fixtures just to see if you can, or, in the absence of ceiling fixtures, they can be just as well thrown into wastebaskets.

Paper clips are very good for making electrical connections, and there is hardly anything better for mending old raincoat pockets. They are also very good for hatband ornamentation, if you care for that sort of thing.

Paper clips are nice and shiny, pleasant to the touch, and make a cheerful sound when rattled in their little cardboard box. But alas! the box is so often empty, and somehow all the paper clips have found their way into a little rats' nest with rubber bands, stamps with no glue on them, bits of eraser, broken leads from mechanical pencils, old pen points, little round reinforcements for loose-leaf paper, and a cough drop or two. There they have quietly rusted and accumulated nasty little globs of dust and tobacco crumbs and there you have to leave them because who'd want to touch *that* mess?

Now you can go hunt for a pin or a stapling machine. If the worst comes to the worst, you can tear the corners of the papers and fold them together, or in a case of utter desperation you can go to the stationery store and buy a brand new box of shiny paper clips. Or, as is more often the case, you can spend the rest of the day running around the house or the office as the case may be asking plaintively, "Has anyone got a paper clip?"

Well, *has* anyone?

String

String is very long thin limp stuff that comes all wound up in balls. Some people save pieces of string that come tied around packages, while others heedlessly throw it away and then when *they* have to tie a package, they're in trouble. On the other hand, the piece of string that you have saved is never exactly the right length for your needs. It is three inches too short. Now *everybody* is in trouble.

String is very important because the post office clings to old fashioned ideas such as that parcels must be tied with string and not stuck with Scotch tape, which is just as well anyway, because the Scotch tape holder is empty.*

* The best solution now is to hide the package in the hall closet, behind the galoshes and sorrowfully tell the prospective recipient it was lost in the mail.

String is thinner than rope, but thicker than thread. If, when you tie up a bundle, the string breaks, you have made a mistake—what you needed was rope.

String is what you hold broken things together with while you look for a pin to stick in the wrong end of the tube of glue because the glue has hardened in the right end.

If you're going to make a cat's cradle, what you most want is a good piece of string. The only trouble with that is that after you've made the cat's cradle, the fish pond, the sidewalk, and the thing that comes after the sidewalk, you're stuck, because you can't make anything out of that one.

You can crochet string or knot it into all kinds of objects. You can. Not me. I haven't got a crochet hook. And anyway, I don't need a doily. I just need a little piece of string to tie up this little package. Here, just put your finger on this a minute, will you?

Garters

A garter is a small round piece of elastic that doesn't hold up stockings. It was invented by Queen Elizabeth or Sir Walter Raleigh—maybe William the Conqueror—someone like that.

Men wear them below the knee, while women wear

them above the knee.* Some men wear them on their sleeves, but this is silly as the word itself means "bend of the knee" and comes from the Old Norman French "gartier."

While most women wear garters around their legs, the Queen of England wears hers over her shoulder. I can't explain this, and I don't know what keeps her stockings up.

At one time it was *de rigueur* for men to wear garters, but nowadays a lot of them are just sloppy. Some men's socks have built-in garters, which must all be very hard on the garter manufacturers who can now consider themselves the unfortunate victims of technological advancement.

Ladies' garters are pink or blue, sometimes black, often ruffled or beribboned. However, this in no way improves their effectiveness. And while men are permitted to go around with their socks falling down, it is still not considered absolutely *soignée* for ladies to do the same. In this regard, women have not yet achieved equality with men, in spite of having gained the vote. While at the polls, it is essential that a lady's stockings stay up.

Round garters come in two sizes. Too tight and too loose. Between the force of gravity, the weight of the stocking, and the incontrovertible fact that the leg tapers toward the knee, the garter is bound to slide down. Some engineer ought to give this matter some thought. I've given it some thought but nothing has resulted. This is what usually happens with my thoughts anyway.

*Anthropological note: This is one of the ways the sexes in human beings can be distinguished.

Which is probably why my name isn't Copernicus or Galileo or Newton or anything. Of course nobody tries to burn me at the stake, so on the whole it may be a good thing. On the other hand if somebody doesn't figure out a way to keep my stockings up, I might be better off at the stake anyway. What is the use of life with wrinkled stockings?

Newspaper

Newspaper is great big white sheets of paper covered with small printing, intended to communicate to some people the foolish things that some other people have done. It is delivered to the front door every morning so that you can start the day happy. It costs just five cents and goes very well with coffee and rolls.

After it has provided you with a half-hour's worth of things to snort at, it can be used to wrap up a fish, if you have a fish to wrap up. (However it is not very good for wrapping up a white pleated chiffon nightgown.) It will serve to empty the vacuum cleaner, line the garbage pail, train a puppy, and pack china in barrels if you happen to be moving. (And if you're training a puppy, moving is a good idea.) Shredded, it makes a fine lining for a box for a cat to have kittens in. It can be cut into paper dolls, made into hats, boats, and birds. Torn to bits, soaked, and mixed with paste it becomes papier-mâché from which hideous ash trays, vases, bowls, etc., can be made.

If you're a hobo, you can make blankets, sweaters, and shoe soles from newspaper or use it to start a fire.

You can put newspaper over a broken window until the glazier comes, or you can put it over your new hat in a sudden rainstorm.

"Spread a newspaper on the floor before you start," is the single most-used admonition in the English language.

The newspaper is also used to check up on the accuracy of the late evening news reports on radio and television. You listen at eleven o'clock, and you say, "It *can't* be true!" Then you pick up your newspaper the next morning, and you say, "It *is* true!"

A newspaper also tells you what day of the week it is. Newspaper is useful.

Paper Bags

A paper bag has a hole in the top. Sometimes it has a hole in the bottom too. Oh well.

You put things in paper bags. You can put anything you like in yours. Of course if it's too heavy or too sharp, the bag will rip and whatever it is that you have put in will come out again.

It doesn't look nice to carry paper bags. I don't know

why. Of course if you're a housewife bringing home groceries, you can probably get away with it. But if you're a gentleman walking on Fifth Avenue with a beautiful girl in a sable coat on one arm, it isn't *comme il faut* to have a paper bag in the other.

If you're a beautiful girl in a sable coat walking on Fifth Avenue, you shouldn't carry a paper bag either. Here, let me take it. My stocking seams are twisted anyway. For heaven's sake, what have you got in here? Oh, it was jelly apples wasn't it. I guess I should have put one hand on the bottom.

People who work in supermarkets know things about paper bags. They can lift them recklessly by the top and nothing happens. But when you get home and try the same trick suddenly there are smashed eggs, bruised oranges, and olives with their pimientos coming out all over the floor, and there you stand with two little bits of brown paper in your hands, murder in your heart, and butter on your new suede shoes.

Paper bags that say "Saks Fifth Avenue" on them are more chic than paper bags that say "Bloom's Delicatessen" if you must carry one. It is sad that you can not buy a new dill pickle at Saks Fifth Avenue though, and if you insist on taking home pickles, you'll just have to give up trying to look chic.

For some reason, it is not only all right to carry a hat box, it is even quite smart. So perhaps you could save some hat boxes from a good store, and carry your pickles around in that. If you carry home a new hat in a paper bag, there is no hope for you.

Paper bags however are quite permissible while strolling about with children. Everyone knows that considerable truck must be carted about wherever there are children, all their little gummy candies and sticky toys with one wheel missing, and the children are too clever to cart it about themselves. They have all they can do to hang on to the one remaining mitten. Besides, only a madwoman would try to appear *soignée* within twenty feet of a child. The sticky comes off. (Here dear, just put that half-eaten caramel-nut-nougat-chocolate-marshmallow bar in this paper bag. Mommy will carry it for you sweetness before you get it well rubbed in your new coat.)

In some parts of the country a paper bag is called a sack, but this is a regionalism I cannot condone. A paper bag is a paper bag.

Nice Kitty, Go Away

The Olden Times

My children, like all children, love to hear about the bygone days when Mommy and Daddy were little. They sometimes express doubts about our veracity, though, because it is so hard for them to imagine the rigors of life in the olden times before they were born.

For instance, I've told them of the clocks and watches that actually had to be wound up by hand each day, and I've told them about the sewing machines that only sewed forwards. I have tried to describe the labor and toil of Venetian blinds whose tilting cords got uneven because there was no mechanical device to keep them even; and they simply refuse to believe that we actually had to press a button to make the pilot light on the range reach the burner when we turned on the gas. "Just imagine!" they say in wonderment.

I've told them about old-fashioned razors and razor blades, and I've told them how Daddy used to have to unwrap the new blade from its paper, open the razor, take out the old blade, put the new one in, and then twist the handle to close the razor again. "Goodness," say the children, "what hard lives people had then!"

I've told them of our toil with shoe polish that needed rubbing and silver polish that needed scrubbing. And

I've told them how, in the old days, we did our laundry with soap. "How in the world did you ever manage?" they ask.

I told them about my first vacuum cleaner, before they were born, that had a dust bag that had to be removed and emptied; about the clothes drier with no chimes to tell you when it was all finished, and the ice-cube trays that actually had to be removed and emptied and then be refilled by *hand*.

I told them about baking a cake by sifting flour and baking powder and salt, and creaming butter and sugar, and adding eggs and vanilla, but they couldn't grasp the idea. I told them how we brewed coffee and tea in pots, and bought vegetables fresh from the ground with the leaves still on and the dirt still clinging to them, but they thought I was joking.

Once I told them about milk that wasn't homogenized, and explained how we used to have to shake the bottle before pouring out the milk. They both came and put their arms around my neck. "Poor Mommy," they said with tears in their little eyes, "how hard you had to work in the olden times!"

The other day I was telling them about cigarette packages whose cellophane wrappings had no little red strip to pull. "Well," they said, "now you've gone *too far*. Now we know you're making it all up."

Through Darkest Coat Closet with
Butterfly Net and Milkman

I'm physically exhausted and emotionally drained. I have been engaged, for the last twenty-four hours, in a hamster hunt.

My youngest son was recently awarded, as a prize for marked bravery and gallantry during a minor operation for the removal of a piece of wood from his neck (and for heaven's sake, let's not go into how a child manages to get a piece of wood in his neck), a Syrian Golden Hamster. At least that's what the lady in the store said he was. This animal, who was promptly named Maxie as a compromise measure (we not being altogether certain whether Max or Maxine would be suitable), is an amiable little beast requiring little attention—a fortunate coincidence, as that is what he gets.

This animal ordinarily resides in a metal cage on my son's bureau. The cage has a little door that slides up and down, and the hamster soon learned to push the door up with his nose and escape. Escape involved falling from the top of a three-foot bureau but never seemed to result in any damage to the hamster. However as we also have a cat, the thought was harrowing.

We rigged up a little wire arrangement that made it impossible for the hamster to open the cage door and breathed easy again—for a while. Then yesterday, someone—I wouldn't like to mention any names—forgot to replace the wire after showing off the hamster to a friend, and Maxie was off again.

In case you have little acquaintance with hamsters, they are animals about the size of a small mouse with lots of fluffy fur, hardly any tail, huge cheek pouches, and very sharp teeth. He is probably a full three ounces, tail, teeth, fur, and all.

We live in a big old-fashioned ten-room house, not counting cellar and attic, with lots of nooks and crannies, stair wells, hallways, old disused floor hot-air registers that lead nowhere—in short, if you stood still and tried to think where you would go if you were a lost hamster the result would be bewildering. Especially when you consider that the hamster's sharp little teeth can gnaw through anything and make a nice little nest in places where nice little nests seem impossible.

He could have been inside a mattress or the pillows of the couch or snuggled into some stored blankets, or in among the books, or in somebody's bureau drawer, or lost forever down the hot-air ducts. He could have been safely tucked away in a galosh or a camera case. He even could have snuggled down in our wall insulation.

Meanwhile, our cat, who suffers from the delusion that she is a great huntress, and who also suffers from constant and intense hunger while waddling around between meals, was roaming restlessly through the house.

I chewed my fingernails and started a posse, consisting of my husband (who was trying to work), the milkman who happened by at an inopportune moment, the mailman who was impressed into service when he came to deliver the bills, and a man who came to install a new water meter. I had another man there too, but I don't know who *he* was. We linked hands and started in the attic.

Six hours later, exhausted and thirsty, we wound up in the cellar, hamsterless.

All the helpers turned out to be quitters and deserted. Hours passed. We were afraid to sit down. We were afraid to walk. We eyed the cat nervously to see if she still looked hungry.

My son was not alarmed. He had already counted up the money in his piggy bank and decided he had just enough to buy a new hamster. Furthermore, he figured, *if* he bought a new hamster, and *if* Maxie then turned up, and *if* the new hamster turned out to be a male, and *if* Maxie was a female, and *if* they mated, and *if* Maxie had babies, and *if* Mommy would chip in for another cage, he would then be in the hamster business, and there was no telling how much money he would earn with which to buy more and more and more hamsters. It was terrifying.

That evening we had guests. We alerted them to the situation and urged caution in sitting. Sometime during the evening, Maxie simply appeared. He (or she) strolled into the living room, calm, relaxed, and unconcerned. His fur was not even ruffled.

But alas, freedom had gone to his head, and when we tried to pick him up to return him to the safety of his cage, he scooted off to another room and hid in a bookcase.

"What you need," remarked a guest, "is a butterfly net."

"Of course!" I said. "How clever of you." And I brought the butterfly net, my husband promptly captured Maxie and put him in his cage, and carefully wired the cage door down.

What I want to know is, what kind of a house *is* this, where hamsters get lost in bookcases, and when somebody says, "Get a butterfly net," there just happens to *be* a butterfly net right handy?

I'm turning in my marriage license and resigning.

Nice Kitty, Go Away

The fact that we have three cats does not necessarily prove that I am a cat lover. It merely proves that the little boy next door's cat had a lot of kittens and that we were spineless enough to accept the gift of two females and that nature then took its course and presently we had seven kittens of which we were only able to foist off six on unsuspecting friends. A hasty trip to the vet precludes the possibility of a recurrence of this disaster, but here I am, a woman who merely tolerates animals, with three of them.

They are not pretty cats. They are a sort of indeterminate old stripey type of alley cat.

They are not particularly smart cats except insofar as

they have managed to inflict themselves on me and get fed two hearty meals a day plus gleanings from the children's cereal bowls in the morning.

They are not particularly clean cats. They have, to be honest about it, fleas.

They are not particularly active cats. We have never had mice, so I don't know if they'd be good mousers, but I doubt it. They are willing, occasionally, to chase a small bird or mole in a desultory way, and they look at squirrels as if they really meant to chase them and might even get around to it one of these days. Indoors I *have* seen them snap at a fly that flew right past their noses, but what they do best is curl up on a cashmere sweater or a hand-crocheted afghan or a down comforter. When they feel the need for exercise, they find it handily by sharpening their claws on the living-room upholstered furniture. My husband made them a de luxe scratching post out of a log, a scrap of carpet, some bells, some bits of yarn, and a dash of catnip, but they have never used it. They prefer the couch. Sometimes they use the legs of a fine antique table. When they weary of that, they go around and unplug all the lamp cords, the favorite being the one that's plugged into an extension cord behind the couch so that we have to move all the furniture to get at it.

These cats that live in my house are nameless. That is, I have a few private names for them but nothing you could call them by right out loud. The little boy next door called his first cat "Snuggles" and his second cat "Ritzy." It is not pleasant to live next door to a boy who is out every evening calling his cats, "Snu-u-u-ugles, Ri-i-i-itzy," especially at mealtime, and it was our wish to avoid such an occurrence in our own home. Therefore, when our little boys thought up names like "Benjamin Franklin" and "Chrisptoher Columbus" for our cats, we put our feet down. However, we were then unable ourselves to think up anything better. My husband, who fancies himself a humorist, finally hit on "Fido" and "Towser." He thought this entertaining. But I was the one who was going to be doing most of the calling, and I was damned if I was going to stand on the front porch in plain view and call, "Here Fido, here Towser," and then have two female kittens come running. No, sir, not me. So I called them "Here, Kitty," and that is their name. Each of the seven kittens was called "Here, Kitty," until we got rid of them. When we failed to get rid of the seventh and finally faced the fact that he was here to stay, there was some talk of calling him "Tiger" but it never amounted to anything.

They do come running when I call them. "Run" is perhaps not exactly the word for it. I call and a few seconds later three blurry gray objects go hurtling past me into the house and pile up in a heap on the hall rug. They unscramble themselves into three separate cats again and go tearing through the house into the kitchen, slide across the linoleum floor and crash into a heap against the cabinets. For it is neither love nor intelligence that brings them galloping home at the sound of my voice. It is just one thing—food. These cats of mine think of nothing but food, care for nothing but food, live for nothing but food. All day long Here Kitty, Here Kitty, and Here Kitty lie around on our best chairs or out in the back yard on a nice soft pile of leaves, waiting for me to call. Once in a while they turn up in the kitchen and stand around and mew. They're too fat now, but I'm afraid to cut down on their food. If they get this hungry with too much to eat, what would they do with just enough? Still, the jostling and crowding at the feeding dish probably gives them a bit of exercise anyway. I used to hear about cats being dainty and taking tiny little bits of food and then wandering off to clean their whiskers before taking another delicate little bite. Ours aren't like that. They stand around the dish, feet planted wide apart to brace themselves against shoves, and dig in, snorting and snarling and kicking and shoving and glaring at each other, and each accusing the other of taking more than his share, and enough food for ten cats is gone in thirty seconds. Then they go off to recline languidly on cashmere sweaters till the next meal call.

Fat—I'm telling you it's a disgrace. It's getting so I'm ashamed to be seen on the same porch with them. They waddle.

Every once in a while I think about the six innocent people who were the recipients of our six kittens and I am overwhelmed by remorse. But I try to comfort myself by thinking of the mother of the little boy next door who walks around looking people straight in the eye and acting as if she were perfectly innocent.

But I am not so stricken with remorse that I wouldn't —say wouldn't *you* like a darling little kitten, a sweet little ball of fluff, affectionate and smart as a *whip* and absolutely no trouble at all to take care of? You wouldn't? Oh.

Story for the Slicks

Carol Saunders brushed her thick mop of chestnut hair off her forehead with long, nervous white fingers. *How am I going to tell Jim?* she thought. *How can I tell him?* She thought of Jim's long, lean jaw, his dark tousled hair, and his crooked grin. *Oh, Jim, Jim—* [Opening paragraph plunges you right into the story with all its intense passion and suspense.]

But I mustn't think about that now. I'm so tired, she thought wearily, and the thin fingers twined nervously in the thick hair. She stood up suddenly and went into the bathroom, and she noticed dully that the faucet was still dripping. *I'll have to get Jim to fix it,* she thought automatically. [The homey touch.]

Determinedly, she turned on the cold water full force and let its clean sparkling freshness flow over her thin white wrists, and then she leaned over and dipped up the water with her slim hands and felt the sharp cold on her hot face. She dipped pads of absorbent cotton in the water and bathed her burning eyes, and she brushed out her hair with long, soothing rhythmic strokes, away from her forehead. [Beauty hints.]

She surveyed herself in the mirror. She saw the white, pointed face and the hair that seemed almost too heavy for the slim neck. It hung round her shoulders in a

151

thick mass. "It's as soft to touch as a spaniel's ears," Jim always said. The lashes around the wide gray eyes were stuck together in dark points with little beads of the cold water still clinging to them. And the lower lip of the full crimson mouth was quivering. [Important that heroine be described, but not too specifically. Sprinkle liberally with "slim" wherever possible. Helpful if heroine can be made to whip in and out of tight sweaters.]

Tomorrow, she thought wearily, twisting and untwisting the long, nervous fingers. *Let tomorrow be time enough to tell him. I'm so tired today.* [There has to be at least one sentence starting with "let."]

She moved swiftly, with the easy flowing walk that Jim loved, and stood awkwardly for a moment in the living room. The late afternoon sun made a brilliant, warm golden splash on the center of the soft green carpet. *It's so quiet,* she thought, *and it seems almost strange to be here, in this house, now.* [This doesn't mean a thing, but it almost sounds as though it does, doesn't it?]

She thought suddenly that it was getting late, and Jim would be home soon. She went into the kitchen and leaned on the cool enamel table. The kitchen was bright and sunny with yellow walls and crisp curtains with appliquéd tulips. [Interior decorating hints are absolutely necessary.]

She caught herself humming a tune—"Star Dust," she realized suddenly. Their song. *Oh, Jim, Jim,* she thought, *remember how it was that night on the top of the bus, and it was so cold and clear, and I could feel the roughness of your coat against my cheek!* [Stir in a little nostalgia.]

And you were laughing because the clean cold wind

kept whipping my hair across your face. Ah, we had fun.
[Always change paragraphs at every possible opportunity, regardless of the meaning. Be sure heroine talks and thinks like a heroine, as opposed to a human being.]

And suddenly the small white face was down on the cold enamel table and bitter sobs shook the slim shoulders. [Got another "slim" in. Good!]

Then she straightened up with determination. *That's enough of that, Carol Saunders,* she thought, and she threw back the slim shoulders and lifted the little pointed chin. [A little pointed chin is always good too—tears at the heartstrings.]

I think I'll make some blueberry torte, she decided, and she glanced at the clock to see if there would be enough time before dinner. There would be, and she started working swiftly; she thought happily, *Jim always loves blueberry torte.* [Always be specific about food. A good recipe never hurts either.]

She deftly creamed a quarter of a cup of rich yellow butter and a tablespoon of sugar in the blue bowl, and added one egg yolk and a little salt and flour. [This is the most complicated recipe I could find in the *Settlement Cook Book*—it ought to be a killer.] She patted and pressed the dough in the shining greased pan (or spring form) with her slim quick fingers till it was a quarter of an inch thick, and placed it in the gleaming refrigerator overnight. Then she filled it with any desired Fruit Mixture, and baked.

Then, still humming to herself, having lined the bottom and sides of a spring form with Muerbe Teig No. 1, page 377, she sprinkled it with bread crumbs, added one quart of blueberries (*How ripe the berries are!* she thought, and she ate one, slowly savoring its sweetness), sprinkled it with one quarter of a cup of sugar (*How white the sugar is!* she thought unexpectedly), and cinnamon and two tablespoons of lemon juice. Over all she dripped the yolk of an egg beaten with three tablespoons of rich yellow cream. She baked it in the hot oven for fifteen minutes, then reduced the heat to three hundred and twenty-five degrees Fahrenheit.

This time she baked it till the crust was golden brown. *Jim loves it with the crust nice and brown,* she thought.

She sniffed the heavenly smell of the Muerbe Teig No. 1, page 377, and her face was flushed from the heat of the stove and her eyes were shining. She beat four egg whites until they were stiff and stood up in little white crusty peaks, and added powdered sugar. When the torte was ready, crust nicely browned, she spread the beaten eggs and sugar over it, returned it quickly to the oven, and baked it fifteen minutes more at three hundred degrees Fahrenheit. [I wonder if anybody ever tried this.]

While she was waiting for it to be ready, she realized suddenly that she was famished, and she thought, *I'll make pickled herring with lots of sour cream, just the way Jim loves it, and chicken soup with matzos balls, and creplach. And pot roast with potato latkes.* [Always give menus. Memo: Remember to get other cookbook. Feel certain this is not the right cookbook for magazine fiction writer.]

Carol didn't hear Jim's key turning in the lock, and he strode in and stood for a moment in the kitchen doorway, looking at her. Her face was flushed, and one tendril of hair had separated from the chestnut mass and curled over one cheek. [A loose tendril is always good.]

Suddenly she felt his presence, and she turned quickly. He was standing there, grinning that crooked grin that always made her heart turn over. [Crooked grin absolutely essential.] He was at her side with one step, and then he was crushing her to him, and her little white face was pressed tight against the warm roughness of his tweed shoulder. He buried his hands in the thick mass of her hair, and then he tilted her face up to kiss her. *She's so little,* he thought. He was always surprised at how little she was. [This establishes that he is of the necessary height and breadth for a proper hero.]

"Jim, darling," Carol said, "let me get my breath." *(He mustn't suspect, she thought. I'll tell him tomorrow.)* "And darling," she said, "you'd better hurry and wash— dinner's ready."

When they sat down to dinner, she was quite composed again. The tall glasses sparkled against the deep-blue linen table mats that she had made from that old blue linen dress and trimmed with the oyster-white cotton fringe that made a happy design against the polished mahogany. [More housekeeping hints.] The lovely old silver that she had got from Grandmother Stanford on her wedding day gleamed softly. She kept the silver polished with reverent care, and its soft sheen never failed to remind her of Grandmother Stanford's shining white hair that she had carried bravely, like a banner. [Bravely, like a banner—isn't that good?] If only she could be as brave, if only she could have the strength that Grandmother Stanford had had.

Not that Carol Saunders hadn't been brave. She'd

been brave the day that Jim had come home from the Army induction center, rejected. She had been strong then. She remembered how he had come home that day, his shoulders bent, his gray eyes smouldering with helpless rage. "It's no good," he had said, "they won't have me—that ankle—" Carol had known about his ankle—that time it had been broken, but he'd fought on to make his touchdown before he collapsed and was carried from the field. That ankle would never be right —she had known that. And she had been strong. [Naturally, there has to be a football injury.]

But this—this was different.

They finished dinner, and Jim helped her to clear away the dishes.

"Darling," she said, blinking back the tears, "I don't feel like washing the dishes tonight—let's just stack them in the sink, and I'll do them in the morning." She pushed her hair back from her forehead with the funny little gesture that Jim loved.

"Sure, honey," he said, "if you say so. It's certainly no hardship for me."

Carol laughed uncertainly. And then suddenly she knew that she had to tell him. Now.

"Come in the living room," she said. Her heart pounded painfully, and she could feel the pulse beating in the soft part of her neck. "I want to talk to you."

Jim looked puzzled, but he followed Carol into the living room. He sank down on the big soft couch covered with deep red frieze and trimmed with a looped woolen fringe of the palest gray. Carol came and sat close to him. She linked her thin fingers and sat there a moment, looking down at her hands. *I have to tell him now,* she thought. But still she sat there, silently, twining and untwining the long, thin fingers.

Jim sat still as death, waiting. Suddenly he leaned forward and caught both her hands in his big ones. "What is it, Carol?" he said, his deep voice vibrant with sympathy. "What is it?" he said again. "Darling," he added softly, "remember that I love you."

Carol looked up gratefully, and her wide gray eyes filled with tears.

She felt fear, like a cold hand laid across her heart.

And then suddenly she thought of Grandmother Stanford. And she knew then, deep within her, that she could be strong too. She held her little head high, and the gray eyes were shining.

"Jim," she said, "I'm going to tell you straight. I—I—" Her voice broke, but she swallowed and went on bravely in a clear voice. [Now, I believe, if I have learned the method properly, we are at the crux of the story. It just so happens I don't have a good crux on hand at the moment, but I can think one up later. It hardly matters, for the denouement is the same in any case.]

Jim stared at her a moment, unbelief in his honest eyes, his long jaw rigid. She saw a tiny muscle quivering in his temple. The room was very still, and somewhere off in the distance they heard the plaintive cry of a train rushing through the night.

Finally Jim spoke. "Carol," he said, and his voice shook a little, "Carol—we'll be all right. We'll start over, you and I, together."

"Jim!" Carol cried. "Oh, Jim!" She started to cry,

and he wrapped her in his strong arms till she was quiet again. "Oh, darling," she said then. "Darling."

Suddenly she sat up straight. "Jim," she said. "Let's wash the dishes *now*."

My Sister and the Three Fat Pigs

In the past few years it has become more and more noticeable that anyone who has spent some time in an exotic place must have a literary career, and vice versa. Everyone who was brought up in India or China, or who lived in rural France, or traveled around in Indochina or Mexico, is busily writing his reminiscences. I think it's time for mine.

Until I was eight years old I never saw another white family except the Johnsons, who lived on the other side of the *na-go*, which would have been called the kampong, or compound, in the Orient, and they seemed more like part of our own family. Technically, I suppose I *had*, because I was born in Ohio, and we didn't move to French Equatorial Africa until I was nearly three, but I don't remember anything about Ohio except the big leather rocker in the living room. [The admission about Ohio gives a nice touch of simple honesty, I think.]

My father was a chemist, and he was doing experiments with a plant called *nbu* by the natives, *Catalandis rubensa* by the botanists, in the hope that under certain conditions it might turn out to have the properties of rubber—only, he hoped, better. [It might be better to make my father a missionary, but I don't know much about missionaries, and chemists are likely to do almost anything, aren't they?] There was a small, crude laboratory built on to the back of the house, where he and my mother used to work all day, doing everything imaginable to that plant, and some things you couldn't imagine.

The laboratory hardly deserved the name, since there was no running water, no gas, and only the crudest and most essential equipment. When my father needed anything he didn't have, he had a choice of waiting anywhere from six to eight months for it or making it himself. [I guess *that* ought to prove that the place was remote enough.] He usually chose the second, since neither he nor my mother had any special desire to stay in Equatorial Africa any longer than necessary. [I hope I'm attaining the proper unemotional attitude in this story. That's the most important thing.]

Mr. Johnson was a botanist, and he was trying to cultivate *Catalandis rubensa* artificially, to provide my father with enough specimens for his work. He was also trying to learn enough about the plant so that if my father's efforts were successful, they could take the plant back to America and cultivate it in quantity. [*Catalandis rubensa*—wouldn't that be a lovely name for a plant? It sounds so erudite, too.]

The Johnsons had three children, slightly older than my sister and I, but their children were safely in school in Switzerland. My mother was trying to give us the equivalent of a grammar school education, but we all knew that soon the dreaded time would come when we too should have to be sent away. [This is the sort of dull explanatory paragraph used by all the experts in reminiscences of this kind.]

In the meantime, we had M'buna to take care of us. There was no word in the dialect of that region meaning nurse, but M'buna was a close approximation, meaning, precisely, foster mother, and relating chiefly to animals, the word *m'ai-buna* meaning mother. [You simply have to sprinkle the story with bits of exotic languages. It's too bad I don't know one, because making it up is a lot of work.] M'buna had chosen the name for herself, and she laughed out loud each time she said it. I think she was slyly making fun of us poor white children, by implying that we were like little animals, helpless. At any rate, it was apparently a great joke. [You always have to give the natives emotions that you don't quite understand—it shows their inscrutability.]

Our M'buna was not, strictly speaking, a nurse, and she did not care for us in the usual sense at all. My mother would not permit her to prepare our food or bathe us, because she feared that M'buna was not completely sanitary in her methods—a fear that was probably well founded. [The more I think about this, the gladder I am that I was really born and brought up in New York City, even though it did stunt my literary career.]

M'buna's real name was M'n-aiba, which meant "Tall One," and which must have been another joke, for she was not tall at all by our standards but quite thoroughly on the dumpy side. We never used her real name except on very formal occasions, like the yearly bestowing of the salary.

M'buna received the magnificent salary of three pigs a year—on the hoof. Pig was a delicacy she had first tasted with us, when my father once brought a pig home from Nichubi, the nearest town, on his bimonthly trip for supplies and mail. We couldn't very well pay M'buna in money, for she would have had no way of spending it. Previously, she had received her salary in calico, jewelry, and sugar, all rare and wonderful things. [I suppose some stickler for accuracy will discover that pigs, calico, jewelry, and sugar are the principal products of French Equatorial Africa, but I have to take *some* chances.]

It was curious that of all the new foods she tried with us, the canned and preserved meats, vegetables, and fruits that were shipped to us from America, pig was the only thing she really cared for. As for the canned milk that my mother ordered in huge quantities, M'buna had asked a million times what it was, but when my mother explained, M'buna simply didn't believe it. [Those natives are *so* unsophisticated.] She insisted that the milk must have some magic quality which we were keeping secret, or why would my mother make up such a patently untrue tale?

M'buna went home each year when she received her three pigs. We never knew exactly when she would go, or exactly when she would return. [You see? I told you they were inscrutable.] She would simply melt away [melting away is something that all natives of strange places have a great knack for] into the incredible darkness of the M'n-bu-go, or Land of the Tall Plants [and please notice the trouble I've gone to with this language] within several days after receiving her pigs, to walk, my father said, some forty miles to her native village in a clearing on the other side of the jungle. How she did it, with no shoes, no machete, and no supplies other than the three pigs, which presumably she would keep to share, roasted, with her people, we never found out. [I wonder if she's a little *too* inscrutable?] But the pigs must have been fairly tough by the time she got them home. After about a week, she would simply be in the house one morning when we awoke.

M'buna had been hired originally to keep an eye on us children, while our mother and father were working, to make sure that we didn't wander too far off and get lost or eaten by wild animals. Later my mother learned that wild animals don't approach human beings if they can help it, and that the jungle was so thick that without a machete or *kabun* you couldn't travel three yards beyond the clearing. But by the time my mother found that out, M'buna was already a part of the family, and no more dispensable than we were. [There's something funny about that jungle, come to think of it. M'buna always managed to get through it, and my father did get to Nichubi every two months, but when it came to us children—oh, well, jungles are supposed to be impenetrable, and I'm sure to think up an explanation if anyone forces the issue.]

The only thing that could possibly have been called a danger was a certain snake, the *bako-nu,* but there the chief likelihood was that it would scare you to death. Though it was a horrible-looking creature, we knew that it would strike only if attacked, and we learned just to stand still until it slithered away. Its bite was supposed to be fatal, and we knew that the natives collected the poison for their own mysterious reasons, but we never knew of anyone who had actually been bitten. [The snake may seem a little unnecessary, but you can't go wrong with some nice bits of local natural history.]

M'buna would, at certain irregular intervals, disappear for sometimes an entire day, sometimes for several hours, but on these occasions we never found out what she did. My father jotted down the dates on a calendar, hoping to discover some sort of regularity to the disappearances, but he couldn't figure it out. After these short absences, M'buna was quiet for the rest of the day, and didn't even giggle when we called her M'buna or drank our milk.

The last year that we were there, my father decided to buy the pigs for M'buna's salary when they were young, and keep them in the clearing to fatten up. He built a wooden enclosure and brought the little pigs home from Nichubi in the back of the old truck. The pigs were squealing and kicking, and my sister was enchanted. I thought they just smelled bad, but all my sister could see was the little curly tails, and she loved them madly. She was only five and a half then, and almost as chubby and squealing as the piglets.

After that, my sister refused to do anything all day but play with the pigs, a diversion that did not dismay M'buna at all but that disgusted me. The family was satisfied though, because it kept her busy and happy and out of trouble, and the pigs were taken care of almost to within an inch of their lives. [This is just to show how normal we were, even in the midst of all that jungle. American or English families are *always* normal, no matter where they are.]

By the end of the year the pigs had grown marvelously and were fatter and healthier than any pigs we had given M'buna yet. My father was pleased at the success of his plan, for, he said, the pigs had plenty of fat for the long walk home.

My sister had grown desperately attached to the pigs, though they were no longer, even by the wildest imagination, the least bit cute or little. She had assigned singularly inappropriate names to them and cried pitifully when my mother warned her that they would have to go. She couldn't bear to think of their being taken away from her to be killed and eaten, and my mother could hardly drag her away from the sty at mealtimes. She had never had a pet before and knew about puppies and kittens only from a few picture books that had come from America.

When my sister finally realized that she would have to give them up, she decided that she would let them go but never, never to be eaten. So one night she crept out of bed and opened the gate of the enclosure. The next day the pigs were gone all right, but no doubt they were eventually eaten anyway, even if not by a native tribe. [You have to be very careful not to let any emotion creep into this sort of story.]

Father was in despair. The pigs hadn't cost a great deal, but they were a great trouble to bring home, and he didn't want to lose the time it would take to make the extra trip. That night at dinner he asked M'buna if she could wait another month for her pigs, since that would be the time for his regular trip. M'buna said she could not. My father and mother looked at each other, and my sister Pat hung her head. M'buna saw that she was creating a great difficulty in the family. Finally she said that she was willing to come to a compromise. Everybody smiled and breathed easier.

"That's fine," my father said. "You mean you'll wait two weeks, then, for the pigs?"

"No," M'buna said. But having thought the situation over, she had generously decided that she would be willing to take my little sister Pat instead of the three pigs. [Actually this is a little more of a surprise ending than is generally permissible in these stories, but perhaps no one will notice.]

Pat and I were sent away to school in France the very next month. [Wind up with just the right note of understatement.]

[I feel sure I could have had a perfectly fascinating childhood riding around in droshkies with a Chekhovian Russian governess or brooding about in a mosque in my bare feet in Mecca. I might even have worked out something pretty good about a succession of Marias somewhere in Mexico. But the main thing in these stories is to stake out a new territory, and who was ever brought up in Nichubi?]

The Case of the Glass Coffin

⌐▭▭▭⌐ Rutherford J. Gainsfort sat at the big oak desk in his study, his head in his hands. [It should be perfectly plain to any reader of detective stories that Rutherford J. Gainsfort is a doomed man.] His stamp album, open to the page with the famous Japanese lavender [a bit of necessary erudition], lay on the desk in front of him, but Rutherford J. Gainsfort was not looking at it. The ornate jade clock on the mantel pointed to ten minutes to eleven. [This is of no significance whatever, but it sounds as though it might be, and anyway you need a lot of false clues in these things to throw the reader off the track.]

Gainsfort groaned, rubbed his forehead with the knuckles of his right hand, took a crumpled note from the inside breast pocket of his gray flannel sack coat, and smoothed it out in front of him. The note was written on pale gray paper with purple ink, and a faint perfume rose to Gainsfort's nostrils as he smoothed out the creases. [All notes are written on pale gray paper with purple ink and are faintly perfumed. I couldn't say why.]

The handwriting, which he studied carefully for the thirtieth time since he'd received the note three days before, was completely characterless and revealed nothing about the writer. The note said: "Dear Gainsfort, Unless you deliver the Japanese lavender before Thursday night at midnight, you will die."

That was all. The note didn't tell Gainsfort to whom the stamp was to be delivered, or where, or why. [You ought to be consumed with curiosity at this point—I know I am.] For two days he had told himself nervously that it was a joke—a joke in very bad taste, too, damn it, he thought. But now, at almost eleven o'clock Thursday night, he was sure it was no joke, and Rutherford J. Gainsfort was frightened. [They always get frightened too late—that's to make it harder for the detective.]

He got a classified directory from the bottom drawer of the desk, leafed through it quickly till he found what he was looking for, and then dialed.

Martin Canby was still in his office at eleven o'clock Thursday night, but not because he was working. He was sitting at the battered, scarred desk in his office, his feet up, his shoes off, a bottle of Scotch in front of him. [The chief mystery here is: Where did he get the price of the Scotch?]

He had shaved that morning, but he had a heavy black beard that gave him an untidy look even when he was freshly shaved. And he had gray eyes. His eyes were the first thing you noticed about Martin Canby, and most people, especially women, didn't notice much else. [There. That ought to establish him as a tough guy—and fascinating, too.]

The phone rang, and Canby stirred. He didn't pick it up till it had rung four times. [See what I mean? A strong-willed type.] "Hullo," he said. "Oh, Gainsfort, huh . . . Yeah, I've heard of the Japanese lavender [he's erudite, too], but I didn't know you had it. . . . When did you say? Three days ago? . . . Listen, I'm not taking on any jobs tonight, thanks. I'm taking a vacation. . . . A thousand? I really need that vacation, Gainsfort. . . . Hell, I'm no charitable institution. . . . Two thousand? O.K. Keep your shirt on, I'll be right over. Oh, and listen. Listen carefully. Stay in your study till I get there. Don't leave the room, and don't let anyone in. Be there in fifteen minutes." [It's plain that Canby has his suspicions, and there's no telling—he may even have solved the case already.]

Canby hung up the phone, lit a cigarette, took another shot of Scotch, and went out.

He took a cab, and when he arrived at the Gainsfort mansion in the East Seventies, he glanced at his watch. It was almost eleven-thirty. He noted automatically that no lights were visible from the street except a dim lamp in the doorway. He cursed under his breath. [I don't know why—detectives just *do* that sort of thing.] He looked at the house for a moment more, threw down his cigarette, ground it out, and lit another. Then he went to the door.

He paused for a moment before ringing the bell, stooped over, and picked something up from the top step and put it in his pocket. [This is probably an important clue, but I'm certainly not going to tell you what it is. That might give you a chance to figure out the mystery as fast as Canby, and we couldn't have that sort of unconventionality, could we?] Then he rang the bell.

A butler with a face masked of all expression opened the door. [All butlers are expressionless, and hang

168

around looking suspicious, but they never do the murder. They're just there to throw you off the track.]

"Where's the study?" Canby asked.

"Mr. Gainsfort is not at home, sir."

"Listen," Canby said, "cut it out. Gainsfort is home, and he's in his study. He called me. My name is Canby." [Detectives hardly ever call anybody Mister.]

"I'm sorry, sir," the butler said, "but Mr. Gainsfort left word that he wasn't to be disturbed."

Without any warning, Canby's right arm shot out, and in the next moment the butler, still expressionless, was lying on his back on the polished floor. [It seems to me that Canby could have found an easier way to get in, but leave it to a detective to do things in a becomingly tough way.] Canby stepped over him and looked around. He whistled once as he took in the magnificent hall.

He started toward a door under which he saw a thin thread of light, snapped his fingers in annoyance, and went back to the butler's motionless body. He removed some papers from the butler's pockets, looked through them quickly, and put them all back, except one which he put in his own wallet. [Listen, I can't tell you what these things are until after Canby has solved the case. What do you think this is? Literature?]

He went on to the door he thought was probably the study and went in. Gainsfort was slumped over the desk, his arms flung out in front of him, and protruding from his back, just under the left shoulder blade, was a tiny curved jeweled handle. A dark stain spread out around the glittering knife handle. [Blood is always spoken of as "a dark stain."] Canby grunted. [Detectives

169

always grunt when they find their client murdered. I don't know whether this is to show repressed emotion or disgust at the possible loss of a fee.]

He went over to the desk and looked at everything, his gray eyes glinting and the muscle in his left cheek twitching. [In anybody else, a twitching muscle would just be a tic and would belong in the same category as a cold in the head. In a detective, it indicates a mind like a steel trap.] Gainsfort's head rested on the open stamp album, and Canby saw, without any change of expression, that the Japanese lavender was still in place. [Nothing surprises *him*.] The note lay on the table, near Gainsfort's left hand.

Canby went over to the window, pulled back the heavy velvet hangings, and looked out. In the earth of the garden below, there were clear footprints, both approaching and leaving the window. The window was locked from the inside. [If there are footprints outside, you can bet your last dollar the window will be locked from the inside.]

Suddenly Canby heard a slight noise inside the room and he wheeled. A woman was standing in the doorway. She was not, Canby guessed shrewdly, quite as young as you were supposed to think. She was dressed in a white negligee, with a small, high, round collar that gave her a curiously young and innocent air that went not at all with the hair that was a little too blonde and the brilliant purplish lipstick painted heavily on her lips.

"Who are you?" Canby growled. [Detectives growl every bit as often as they grunt. In fact, they rarely sound like human beings.]

170

"I'm—I'm Mrs. Gainsfort," she said hesitantly in a low voice. "Is he—dead?"

"Yeah," Canby said, "he's dead all right. You knew he was dead before you came in here. Why did you ask me?"

"All right, Mr. Canby," she said, almost in a whisper, "I'll tell you everything. I did know he was dead. I—I came in here to ask him something, about ten—no, fifteen—minutes ago, and I found him like this. Mr. Canby, it's no secret that my husband and I didn't get along. I—I was—afraid. So I ran back upstairs and waited." Her voice was almost inaudible as she finished. [I can't help all this repetition. You just have to have it in a detective story. If a character talks in a low voice, you have to mention it every time the character speaks. This is called "character development."] "What are you going to do?" she whispered hesitantly.

Canby sat down on a corner of the desk and picked up the telephone. He dialed, and as he waited for an answer he spoke mildly to Mrs. Gainsfort. [They always talk mildly as the trap springs.] "It was clever," he said. "Except for one thing, I never would have guessed."

From here on the story winds swiftly to its inevitable denouement. Lieutenant Robinson of the Homicide Squad arrives. He isn't stupid exactly, but nobody is allowed to have a mind like a steel trap except the detective. He is no help at all, but that doesn't matter, because Canby's lightning brain has the whole diabolical plot figured out anyway.

Naturally the Japanese lavender has nothing to do

with the murder—it was just to throw you off. As for the glass coffin, well, you have to have a *title*. It probably turns out that the glass coffin is a goldfish bowl containing one dead goldfish which gave Canby all the clues. Or perhaps *The Glass Coffin* is the title of a book found in Gainsfort's bathtub. *I* don't know. In any case, the story winds up with Canby, suddenly and unaccountably articulate (you mustn't carry character development too far in this sort of story), explaining the whole thing to Lieutenant Robinson.

Of course you can't hope to get out of this without hearing any number of versions of the plot: in addition to Canby's account to Robinson, you have to suffer through the criminal's confession, and you can tell, before the book is over, that *somebody* is going to repeat the whole thing to somebody else—but it won't be me.

One thing more: Canby knew *plenty* that I didn't give away, and it may well be that at the very end, as Canby exits, grinning at his cleverness, there will be several items unaccounted for.

The murderer, in case you care, was a man named Pottsworthy, who entered the story as the cab driver.

What Are You Gonna Do?

What's in a Name Plate?

I'm all worn out. I've been scrubbing and polishing. Spring cleaning? No. Closets? No. Silverware, shoes, woodwork? No. I've been polishing up all the manufacturers' names on the fronts of my appliances.

I have a nice modern kitchen, with good equipment and everything designed for easy upkeep. My appliances are porcelain, counters plastic and stainless steel, cabinets baked enamel, floor linoleum, and everything seamless and with rounded corners for easy cleaning. Everything, that is, except the chrome-plated lettering on the front of my range, refrigerator, washing machine, dishwasher, drier, and vacuum cleaner.

The lettering is large, raised, prominent, ugly, and perfectly designed to catch dust, grease, lint, scouring powder, and threads from the cleaning cloths. I like to keep my kitchen clean and shining—and I do, too. Except for those maddening names. To get those clean, you'd have to take a day off and poke in among the letters with little cotton swabs or something. I don't even know if you ever *could* get them clean.

Besides, I object strenuously to advertising on my own belongings. If they want to advertise their ranges and refrigerators, let them buy space for it. Or let them give me the appliances free.

I never heard of a carpet manufacturer weaving his

name down the middle of his carpets, or a dress manufacturer sewing his label on the outside of the dress.
Builders don't affix large signs with their names on the
buildings they have built. Why, then, must I have trade
names shouting at me all over my kitchen and distract-
ing me when I'm baking a pie? I don't like it. Why
can't they tack neat little smooth, *washable* name plates
on the insides of the doors like any other self-respecting
manufacturers?

And in the meantime I wish they'd come and give me
a hand with my polishing. I still have forty-seven letters
to go.

How to Bread a Veal Cutlet
in a Bureau Drawer

This year my spring fever got all out of
hand, and when some friends asked us to join them for
a weekend at their country house, I not only said yes
but had to wipe my chin. My husband, in a rare moment
of sanity, was dubious but finally agreed.

Everything started off beautifully. Our friends with
the house-in-the-country picked us up on a Thursday
afternoon, so we could have a good long weekend, and
we set out gaily. It was a lovely warm day, the sun glowing, the breezes blowing, the cows lowing, the river
flowing, the trees growing, the farmers hoeing and
sowing, tugboats towing, small boys rowing, crows

crowing, people to and fro-ing, slips showing, and—God knowing.

The house was completely charming. Except that the pump was broken, that mice and wasps had been wintering snugly in the beds, that the windows were nailed tightly shut, and that, after we drew water from the well in leaking buckets, we learned that the drains stubbornly and noisily refused to drain, the place was a paradise.

Had it been my house, I would have (a) sent for a plumber, (b) sent for an exterminator, and (c) burned the place down. Our friends decided to paint the kitchen.

And that is how the dishes got into the bathtub, the kerosene stove got into the living room, and I got into trouble.

I ask you, kind reader, in all sincerity, have *you* ever breaded a veal cutlet in a bureau drawer? Here is how you do it. You take your veal cutlet in one hand, and a box of bread crumbs in the other. (Cracker meal will do nicely, too.) You put a little pile of bread crumbs in the bureau drawer. Then, still carrying the veal cutlet (you wouldn't want to put it down on the floor, would you?) you carry it through the living room, through the half-painted kitchen, out onto the porch. You wave the veal cutlet around. "Anybody here seen the salt and pepper?" you ask. Nobody has. Naturally. What do you think this is, you city slicker? You carry your veal cutlet back into the house. "Never mind the salt and pepper," you think, "get on with the breading. Is this Chambord?" You dip your veal cutlet in the bread crumbs in the bureau drawer, and you leave it there while you

177

hunt for an egg. Guess where the eggs are! In the ice-box! Isn't that marvelous? The reason the eggs are in the icebox is not because the icebox is cold, because it isn't. There isn't any ice. (Naturally.) It's because when you close the icebox door, the mice can't get in. It's really all very simple once you get the hang of it. So you get the egg. On your way back through the living room, you find a soup plate that has somehow found its way there, and you break the egg into it. You carry the egg shell out to the back porch, where the garbage pail is. (After all, who'd keep a garbage pail in a living room or a bedroom? Just because you're breading a veal cutlet in there doesn't make it a kitchen, you know.) You come back, pick up the soup plate with the egg in it, and you carry that carefully out to the back porch. Oops! Slop over a little onto your shoe? Never mind, you can scrape it off later. "Has anybody seen the forks?" you ask, but without much hope. Nobody has, but everybody is co-operative, and they all get up and hunt. Sooner or later you decide not to wait any longer, and you gratefully accept your husband's pocketknife, and you beat up the egg with that. Did you ever beat up an egg with a pocketknife? No? Well, never mind. You just do it. Then you carry the beaten egg back into the bedroom, where the veal cutlet is nestling in a pile of bread crumbs in the bureau drawer, and you set the soup plate on the floor. (Isn't it too bad the top of the bureau is covered with Things. It would have made such a dandy work space.) You dip the veal cutlet in the beaten egg in the soup plate on the floor. Ts, ts, bread crumbs in your shoe? Itches, doesn't it. Well, never mind, you can clean them out later. You lift your veal cutlet out of the beaten egg. Now comes the ethical problem. Should you put the veal cutlet back in the bureau drawer? A bit of egg drizzles onto the floor while you decide. Too bad. Well, you can't expect to live the same way in the country, can you. Eventually you decide it's no time for ethics, and you dip the veal cutlet back in the bread crumbs in the bureau drawer. After it's nicely breaded and has set for a while, you carry it gingerly to the stove in the living room. You put it in the one frying pan. The frying pan is too small. Well, one doesn't like to complain, does one. So you just get the penknife again and hack off a hunk—that can cook later perhaps. Meanwhile you can just put it back in that bureau drawer for a while while you look for a time-table.

While you look up trains, you ask yourself a rather interesting question. The country is nice, but is it absolutely necessary?

Ho for the Hot-Dog Stand!

I have been trying hard to forget some advice I saw recently in a magazine. But the more I try to forget it, the more it goes round in my head, moiling and roiling and causing me all kinds of trouble.

This advice, consisting of four sentences, has aroused in me the greatest admiration for the fortitude of the average American stomach. For I must assume that in millions of American homes these sentences have been taken to heart—or rather, to stomach.

The sentences are the following:

"Made-over clothes are often more exciting than new ones; so it is with food. Example: stuff celery with peanut butter and leftover chopped cooked prunes.

"That dab of creamed chicken you don't want to waste is delicious spooned into centers of peachhalves and broiled. Add shreds of cheese if you like.

"Smart way to salvage lemon slices originally cut for tea is to press one on top of each sweet potato patty and broil. Dust lemon with a bit of sugar.

"If all the green pepper strips aren't taken from the relish dish, chill those left and chop next day. Scatter on top of hot cooked cabbage."

It is my belief that advice such as this is going to undermine the American home. I was always under the impression that most Americans were in the habit of saying, "Gee, if I could only have some of Mom's apple pie," or "Boy, what I wouldn't give for some of Mom's roast beef," or "Brother, could I go for some of Mom's spaghetti and meat balls." It is hard for me to revise this impression and replace it with, "Gee, how I'd love some of Mom's celery-stuffed-with-peanut-butter-and-leftover-chopped-cooked-prunes!"

In my case, Mom's *pièce de résistance* was a chocolate icebox cake, so rich you couldn't stand to think about it more than twice a year, but so good it made up for her not being such a good egg scrambler. We weren't fussy eaters, on the whole, though if dinner didn't consist of roast beef or steak and chocolate cake, my father and sister were apt to grumble some. I hate to think, though, what would have happened if Mom had dared to serve

180

celery stuffed with peanut butter and leftover chopped cooked prunes. She had the devil's own time getting rid of leftover roast beef, let alone chopped cooked prunes, or bits of old lemon slices or green peppers. As for dabs of creamed chicken spooned into peachhalves and broiled with shreds of cheese, the entire family, including Mom, would have risen in a body and marched off to the nearest hamburger stand.

I believe firmly that leftovers have a place in the American home. It is only decent that leftover food should be eaten up. But a leftover leftover is not only unappetizing and un-American, but proof, what's more, that the thing couldn't have been much good to begin with, and therefore is hardly likely to be edible at this stage. Either that or Mom is a dope and bought three times as much as she needed, which is foolish and leads to things like creamed chicken broiled in peachhalves. Mom should buy a smaller chicken in the first place and leave the peachhalves alone. That's my advice.

The thing that worries me about all this is that if I know Americans at all, there's going to be an awful lot of celery-stuffed-with-peanut-butter-and-leftover-chopped-cooked-prunes and dabs-of-creamed-chicken-broiled-in-peachhalves left over. The whole idea wasn't my fault to start with, but now that the damage is done, I'm willing to help out with a suggestion. Here it is: Leftover-celery-stuffed-with-peanut-butter-and-leftover-chopped-prunes is delicious minced fine and added to leftover-creamed-chicken-broiled-on-peachhalves-with-shredded-cheese. Add shreds of hot cooked cabbage if you like, and garnish with sweet potato patties.

There! That ought to clean out the nation's overworked iceboxes and give everybody a chance to start off with a smaller chicken and fewer stewed prunes, and get going again on a decent American diet.

Broiled peachhalves indeed!

What Are You Gonna Do?

You cannot make yourself a tomato surprise. You can fill the tomato with chicken salad, tuna fish, crab meat—anything you like. But when you are done, it will not be a tomato surprise. It will just be a tomato filled with chicken salad, tuna fish, or crab meat.

This is too bad. Lots of times, on a hot summer day, I just feel that I would like to have a tomato surprise, and I try hard not to watch when I put in the filling, but if you don't watch, you're likely to put it on the table or the floor instead of into the tomato, and then the cat will sniff at it and get it all messy. So no matter what I do, when I sit down to eat it, I'm not surprised at all. I knew all the time it would have crab meat in it.

I've tried putting surprising things inside it. I tried corned beef hash, vanilla ice cream, and once I even tried putting tomato into it. But *I* wasn't surprised.

It's sad, when you think about it. It's like not being able to see yourself as others see you, and not being able to go forwards or backwards in time, and not having curly hair.

So you just have to go through life waiting for other people to surprise you. And if you want a tomato surprise, you have to eat in a restaurant. Oh well.